What Others Are Saying About this Book . . .

"Knowing precisely what you want—and bringing it about—can be a challenge. In this excellent book, the authors take you on an exciting journey of discovery, one that has you expertly navigate through hidden fears and procrastination so as to embrace passion and adventure in creating your best life. I highly recommend this skill-based book."

—**Shawne Duperon, six-time Emmy-award winner,** *Shawne TV*

"This inspirational book will guide you to satisfying goals, ones that expand and better your life."

—**Debbi Dachinger, syndicated award-winning host**
of *Dare to Dream Radio,* **and bestselling author of**
Dare to Dream: This Life Counts!

"Charmaine and Debra have created the perfect guidebook and repair manual for servicing your most important vehicle: yourself. No matter where you are in your life, the concepts and direction provided in this book will help you get to a better place. It's a must read."

—**Ken Kragen, author of** *Life Is a Contact Sport,*
and organizer of *We Are the World,*
Hands Across America **and**
other historic humanitarian events

"A most useful guide to charting and traversing the many options that lay before you."

—**Suzi Kenyon, Kenyon Communications**

"If you are in a life or career transition you must read *GPS Your Best Life.* In this book, Charmaine and Debra share simple self-analysis questionnaires and real world examples to help you discover and reach desired destinations."

—**April Morris, seen on ABC's hit TV show** *Shark Tank*

"There are a lot of self-help books on the market, but this takes a unique, creative approach to help you figure out where you want to go in your life and how to get there, in an easy, fun, step-by-step manner."

—Christine Belleris, president, Beyond Words, Inc.

"This terrific book shows you how to focus on what you want, clear away obstacles, and chart a course to make your dreams come true. A must-read for anyone who is serious about living a life of purpose and passion."

—Gail Z. Martin, author of *30 Days to Social Media Success*

"A valuable guide to help you think and rethink your next move—personal and professional."

—Jennifer L. Youngs, author of
7 Ways a Baby Will Change Your Life the First Year

"This book is easy to read, easy to understand and simple to follow. And best of all it really works! If you want to be clear about your priorities and know what is important to you, this book is a must read!"

— Lori Raudnask, author of *Persistence Pays:*
How Getting What You Want is Easier Than You Think

"This book packs a powerful message. It puts you in the driver's seat, making you an unstoppable force. If there are any areas of your life where you're not getting the results you want, the answers to achievement can be found in these pages."

—Marilyn Suttle, success coach and author,
Who's Your Gladys? How to Turn Even the Most
Difficult Customer into Your Biggest Fan

GPS YOUR BEST LIFE

CHARTING YOUR DESTINATION—AND GETTING THERE IN STYLE

CHARMAINE HAMMOND & DEBRA KASOWSKI

BETTIE YOUNGS BOOKS

Copyright © 2012 by Charmaine Hammond and Debra Kasowski

All rights reserved, including the right to reproduce this work in any form whatsoever, without permission in writing from the publisher, except for brief passages in connection with a review.

Author photo of Charmaine Hammond and Debra Kasowski by Tracy Grabowski Photography
Cover Design by Tatomir Pitariu
Text Design by Jane Hagaman
Senior Editor: Elisabeth Rinaldi
Publisher: Bettie Youngs Books

Bettie Youngs Books are distributed worldwide. If you are unable to order this book from your local bookseller, Espresso, or online, you may order directly from the publisher.

BETTIE YOUNGS BOOK PUBLISHERS
www.BettieYoungsBooks.com
info@BettieYoungsBooks.com

ISBN: 978-1-936332-26-7
eBook: 978-1-936332-41-0

Library of Congress Control Number: 2010915598
1. Hammond, Charmaine. 2. Kasowski, Debra. 3. Careers. 4. Self-Help.
5. Motivation. 6. Setting Goals. 7. Interpersonal Communication.
8. Self-Image.

Printed in the United States of America

CONTENTS

FOREWORD

I had casually met Charmaine Hammond and Debra Kasowski on a couple of separate occasions, but a workshop I was conducting in Canada brought the three of us together for a formal meeting in October of 2009. Right before that I had received a video testimonial from these two enthusiastic and passionate women in which they shared the successes they had achieved after participating in my Success Principles Tele-Coaching Program, so I agreed to meet with them when the workshop was over. It was wonderful to see two women who were so totally aligned with each other and who were fully living the success principles in their daily lives and, in the process, were empowering others. Charmaine and Debra, whom I now refer to as "the dynamic duo," impressed me with their creativity, their knowledge, their ingenuity, and their commitment to helping others achieve success.

In my career as a transformational speaker, trainer and coach, I have seen many people who want to change their lives; however, most of them have trouble getting started because they have not clearly determined what they want. They often lack any clear sense of their purpose, vision and goals. *GPS Your Best Life* will help you gain the clarity you need and put you on the road toward success. This book is filled with practical techniques and tools to assess where you are in your life right now, how to determine where you want to go, and how to overcome any inertia that may be holding you back from getting started, continuing and completing your journey from where you are to where you want to be. With *GPS Your Best Life*, Charmaine and Debra have created a system that will guide you into taking the right direction so you live an exciting, meaningful and fulfilling life. Above all, Charmaine and Debra will show you how to navigate through life's inevitable roadblocks and obstacles with grace and ease so you can reach your desired destination!

—**Jack Canfield, co-author of** *The Success Principles*™
and the #1 *New York Times* **bestselling**
Chicken Soup for the Soul® series

ACKNOWLEDGMENTS

FROM CHARMAINE

To Christopher, my husband and biggest champion. I am blessed to have you by my side in business, life, and love. To my mother and father, Josie and Ken, for instilling a powerful set of values that have allowed me to live my best life. To my sisters, Adele and Melanie, for your support and for our rich friendship, as beautiful as our most joyful childhood memories. To my mentors, Gary Reid, Lisa Nichols, Patricia Drain: for your mentorship and guidance I am grateful. To my childhood and best friend, Rose Anne. You have always been a grounding force in my life; I treasure always our childhood memories, and rich moments.

FROM DEBRA

To Stephen, my husband and my best friend who has loved, encouraged, and supported me in reaching my dreams. Thank you for being my knight in shining armor. My beautiful and fun-loving children, Krista, Nathan, and Jordan, you inspire me and light up my life. I love you and I am so proud of you for learning to be true to yourself. You are my greatest treasures. To my parents, John and Elizabeth, thank you for your unconditional love and support and in teaching me the importance of living my faith and always believing in my dreams. To my siblings, Jim, John, Michelle, and Andrew, thank you for helping me become the person I am today; I will treasure the special times we have shared in my heart forever. Special thanks to my mentors, Marcia Wieder, Janet Attwood, and Sandra Yancey, for helping me see that I am here for a greater purpose than I anticipated for myself. I am blessed to be surrounded by such incredible thought leaders.

From the both of us

To Bettie Youngs of Bettie Youngs Book Publishers for your continued guidance and support through the writing and publishing journey. Your wisdom helped us create above and beyond in so many ways. Thank you, as well, to your wonderful staff, most especially to senior editor Elisabeth Rinaldi, for her encouragement and expertise in drawing out our stories and of course, for her editing excellence. Thank you to Adrian Pitariu, Jane Hagaman, Christine Belleris and others in helping us bring our book to readers everywhere on the planet.

To Jan King for coaching us through the writing process. We are grateful for the gift of your experience.

To Jack Canfield, our mentor. Thank you for your guidance through the Success Principle Coaching Program, your books, and your support.

To Jo-Ann Vacing, we so appreciate you showcasing our GPS Your Best Life workshops for women entrepreneurs across Alberta.

To all the individuals who have participated in our GPS Your Best Life programs, and for your commitment to living your best life!

INTRODUCTION

At some time in our lives, we've all used a map to find the best route to a destination. Perhaps someone provided you directions or drew you a route. Maybe you have used an Internet application to find the driving directions to a specific location.

Picture this: two friends, Amy and Emma, are visiting a mega-mall for the first time. The mall has an indoor wave pool, mini golf, a skating rink, an amusement park, and hundreds of stores and attractions. You can just imagine its size. As the two friends pull their car into the gigantic parking lot, Amy's eyes widen, her mouth falls open as she says, "Holy smokes! This place is huge. How will we ever find our way around?" As they venture wide-eyed into the mall, they find a directional sign that indicates "You are here" with a little star telling them where in the big mall they are. This will help Amy and Emma determine which direction to take to the stores they wish to visit. Additionally, it provides them with a general overview of where they are standing in context of the big mall. Amy takes note of the stores located closest to the entrance. Without taking note of their bearings, they could have had quite a chore looking for their car in a massive parking lot.

GPS PINPOINTS WHERE YOU ARE

You're probably familiar with Global Positioning Systems (GPS) or might even have a GPS in your car. More and more people are using a GPS to plot and navigate their journeys. In fact, many cell phones and tablets come with a GPS device. A GPS is a satellite-based navigation system that determines your exact location on the planet. Did you know that there are more than 30 satellites in the orbit, some 10,000 plus miles above the earth? Those satellites transmit precise signals, which allow the GPS receivers on earth to calculate and display an accurate location, speed, and time information to the user. The more clearly a satellite can receive signals from your GPS, the more clearly and accurately it can determine your positioning and whereabouts.

Your best life can be established through a similar system. A GPS does not work like a compass where you can stand and orient your position in North, East, West, or South direction; it determines positioning through movement in order to figure out which way to go next. With a GPS, once you input the address or even the broad coordinates of where you want to go, it is likely that you will get to (or very close to) your desired destination. How helpful would it be to have your own internal GPS for your life? A personal GPS which would help you navigate through life's challenges and toward your goals. Having an internal GPS would tell you where you are in relation to where you want to be, and would plot the best route to your desired outcomes. A GPS can also tell you your speed and how long it will take to reach your destination, map out the best route to your destination, and recalculate when you are off course.

Think of your life as a vehicle: you're the driver with your hands on the wheel and this book is your GPS to help you navigate your life. The GPS is just like that "You are here" sign in the mall—it shows where you are in relation to where you want to go, and the different routes to get there.

This book is your personal guide to getting positioned for success in your best life and will get you on your way to new beginnings, whether that means going back to school, changing careers, starting a business, or making a change in a relationship. The journey starts with knowing where you are right now and seeing the big picture of where you want to go. You can begin your journey at any time. It is a matter of making the decision. The decision is: "What do I want my *best* life to look like?"

Chapter 1

Where You Are Right Now

"If you don't know where you are going,
how can you expect to get there?"
—Basil S. Walsh

Just like a trip to the mall, any journey you take in life begins with getting ready. You probably know firsthand that sometimes it takes more time and energy to get ready for an event than to enjoy the actual event. Graduations, weddings, retirement parties, and baby showers are all great examples. Even the process of getting children ready to head out to a soccer game takes planning, time, and energy. Without preparation, you could arrive at the game missing what you need. Life is no different. It is easier to know where you want to go and which route you will take, when you know where you are starting from and make a plan to get to your destination.

At this moment, you may be in a situation where you are quite content. Chances are however, if you have your hands on this book, you are looking to improve some area of your life, or maybe you just want a change but aren't exactly sure what.

There's an ancient Buddhist proverb that says when the student is ready the teacher will appear. You've picked up this book, indicating you're ready, and we are here to help you along your journey. You may not know exactly what your final destination is right now, but once you take a look at your current life situation you will be ready to move forward and decide what you want your best life to look like.

Even though many people are not certain where they want to go, most people desire a better life. There are times when we find that certain areas of our lives no longer serve us, and we realize we need a change. For many, the thought of change and the transition it entails can be overwhelming. Whether you purchase a house, move, start a new job, become a mother, or retire, all these events and transitions can be scary and overwhelming because so often the results are unknown. So many people are discouraged about their status quo, but are uncomfortable and even resistant to change. Fear of change can hinder a person's success, unless of course the person can turn fear into focus!

Fear of change can hinder a person's success, unless of course the person can turn fear into focus!

When Jenny and her husband David got the unexpected news of David's transfer, they faced a big decision. They loved their home, their children were settled and doing well in current school; David and Jenny had many close friends both through his work, and in their neighborhood; they had pictured themselves retiring in their home. David was excited about the potential for his career yet dreaded uprooting the family again; this would be their second move in five years. Jenny was showing some negativity with the prospect of moving, and this resulted in arguments and strain on the family.

As Jenny and David explored what was best for their family, the conversation quickly turned to reviewing their personal values and priorities. While this wasn't an easy or comfortable conversation, it was critical in helping them decide what they would do next. They brainstormed and listed their options and as they did so, it became apparent that they had more options than they had initially realized. They also learned that there was more to consider than simply the decision to take the transfer or not. Rather than feeling fearful and hesitant about the possibility of moving, they started feeling more focus toward making the right decision and felt energetic about the challenge ahead of them.

Sometimes you need to defer a good opportunity to receive a great opportunity.

As Jenny and David made use of their GPS tool kit, they got crystal clear on their vision for their family. They identified some of their key priorities as: being close to family and friends, ensuring a quality education for the children, investment in extra-curricular activities, providing stability for the children. Additionally, both Jenny and David's parents were getting older, and the couple wanted to spend as much time as they could with their parents and be immediately accessible to them. David was finishing up his MBA, and financial stability was also a priority. After deliberation, the couple decided that now was not the time to accept the transfer offer. When they turned down the transfer offer, they had no idea how the future would play out, but they did know that their decision was in line with their vision and values. A year later, a new opportunity in their area surfaced, offering more money and perks than the previous offer. Sometimes you need to defer a good opportunity to receive a great opportunity.

A GPS makes life easier than going without a road map or an instruction manual; not only helping you navigate and chart your course, but helping you when you're lost. When traveling in a vehicle, it can be unnerving, and perhaps frightening to get lost and not find your way. The same is true in life. When we think we're lost, we feel overwhelmed. By having your own GPS, you will be able to navigate through busy and challenging times, when priorities get lost in the shuffle or when you need to locate the resources that can help you the most.

As you start brainstorming ideas and planning out your best life, you too will likely notice a shift in your focus and energy level. Your newfound energy, will allow you to explore available options, and it will be easier to focus on the opportunities the road ahead offers you.

We all have within us a personal GPS. Often though, it's not turned on. Turning it on is the step to discover why you are making a commitment to change. Knowing what you want, feeling emotionally connected to your dream or vision for yourself, and having the mindset to succeed will position you for success.

As you read through this book you will discover how to activate your GPS and *get positioned for success.* Your GPS is built on three navigational points: getting clear on what you want, mapping the journey, and overcoming the obstacles that get in the way. When these three navigational points are in sync, great things happen.

To start tapping into your GPS, the first navigational point is to get *clear* on what it is you want. Think of this process much like putting on a pair of glasses to help you see crystal clear and to bring everything into sharp focus.

THE GPS CHECKUP QUESTIONNAIRE

Let's take a GPS quiz to help you get clear about your values, attitudes, and wants, as well as give you ideas for where to focus your energy at the start of your journey. This quiz may also help you identify some of road marks you'll want to reach while mapping your plan.

This questionnaire is your own personal checkup, like an all-points diagnostic done on your vehicle when you take it to the repair shop for a tune up. This self-checkup will provide insight and information about how ready you are right now to turn on your GPS and create your best life.

It is like a snapshot in time, the "You are here" sign for this moment in your life. You can take this checkup whenever you want, so if you take it today and want to compare notes three months down the road, go for it. We do recommend that you complete the questionnaire once a year to make sure you are still on course.

As you work through the questions, don't feel like you have to overanalyze your answers. Don't worry about whether your answers are correct: there is no right or wrong here. You cannot fail. The questionnaire is all about assessing your current situation. The only thing that is required is that you be honest with yourself—an important skill to develop when using your GPS. This is a great place to begin putting honesty and self-awareness into practice. How ready you are to make change in your life depends on how well you know yourself and what you want. So listen to your inner voice, your intuition, your wisdom—whatever term you like best. Simply trust in yourself. You will know when you are on the right course.

The results of this checkup will vary depending on where you are on your journey. When life is at an all-time high, our responses will differ from when we might be facing difficulties or challenges. This checkup will allow you to adjust your route, so that you can handle anything that comes your way.

Personal Diagnostics

Score yourself for each of the questions that follow, using a rating scale of 1 to 3, where:

1   All my fluids are topped off and ready to go. This area is a real strength for me. There is not a lot of need for improvement. "This is an area where I am in high gear!"

2   My fluids may be low, and it's time to schedule a service check. This can be an area of strength, but something I still need to work on; I am inconsistent in this area. "I have good days and bad days, but mostly good."

3   Engine warning light is on. I am running on empty. This is an area I need to improve. "I am really a great work in progress."

1	2	3	
			Attitude/Mindset
			I am generally a positive, hopeful, and optimistic person.
			I take responsibility for my accomplishments (successes) and my mistakes. I know I can't control what happens, but I can control how I deal with it.
			Generally I can work through worry and fear and do not let them hold me back.
			My home and work areas are mostly organized and clutter free.
			I take responsibility for myself, my attitudes, and my actions.
			I pay attention to my intuition (gut instinct) and the signs around me that tell me when something is not right.
			I am able to say "no" and set boundaries to others' requests without feeling guilty.
			I tend to look at why and how something new will work instead of why it will not work.

			Relationships
			I typically surround myself with encouraging, supportive, and positive people. My closest friends and colleagues are cooperative passengers in my life, not backseat drivers with many opinions on how I should drive (or live my life).
			I am able to discuss difficult or controversial topics with others without avoidance or becoming overly defensive.
			When I don't see eye-to-eye with someone, I am still able to openly listen to the other person's perspective, even if I don't agree.
			When conflict or disagreement occurs, I am able to discuss and resolve it with minimal impact on the relationship.
			When issues arise in relationships and are then resolved, I am able to let them go (I do not hold onto resentments or keep bringing up the past).
			I am able to build long lasting and meaningful relationships.
			My relationships are based on strong foundations of mutual respect and trust.
			I am comfortable sharing my goals, aspirations, and dreams with others.
			When others tell me about their dreams, I am interested in listening and exploring how I can help, instead of looking at how it relates to me.
			Personal Growth
			I have a clear sense of what I want to do with my life.
			On a daily basis, I choose actions that support my commitments to myself, and I honor them.
			I can list at least five things that I am passionate about (things I love to do).
			My personal image (physical, mental, and communication style) is important to me. I think, speak, and dress for success.
			When others provide me with feedback, I am able to listen without jumping in and defending myself or blaming others.
			I am able to accept and appreciate positive feedback and compliments received from others without minimizing or doubting their intent.

			I take healthy steps to manage my stress.(For example, I keep my energy up by getting enough sleep.)
			I have a clearly defined set of goals (with timelines and action plans).
			I ask for help when I need it.
			I can accept help graciously when it is offered.
			I perform random acts of kindness without any expectation of something in return.
			I have dealt with unfinished business that required attention or was holding me back.
			I can identify three areas, where I have experienced personal (or professional) growth in the past year.
			I am able to identify two habits that I need to change to bring about better results.
			Add up how many 1s, 2s, and 3s you had for each column.

Congratulations! You've completed the all points diagnostic on the vehicle that is your life. Time for the mechanic to tell you what it all means.

The GPS Checkup Score Card

There were thirty-one questions in all. If you scored mostly ones, congratulations. You are well on your journey to GPSing your best life. The information in this book will help you find the shortest and most beneficial route to success. It will also provide you with tools to navigate through any future bumps in the road.

If you scored mostly twos, you are like most people. You may know what you need to do, but you sometimes struggle with the challenges that get in the way or how to go about something. Being consistent is often difficult. Think of this book as the car manual you keep in your glove box, always there when you need it and anytime you have questions.

If you scored mostly 3s, do not panic. Keep your hands on the wheel, and your eyes on the road. We all experience times when achieving our best requires more effort than we thought. As you keep your eyes on the destination. This book *is* your roadmap.

When you look over the results of your responses, what became clear for you? What surprised you? Did anything alarm you? If so, why? What did your responses tell you about where you are now and where you'd like to be?

Here are a few extra questions to guide this self-reflection:

- What surprised me most was…
- What did I see from the results that I already intuitively knew?
- What new insight was highlighted for me?
- What strength(s) did I discover?
- What are some areas for improvement or growth?
- What one area will I put energy and time into? Why?
- Would asking for support help me out? If so, who could I ask?
- What are my gifts and talents that I can share with others?

Keesha's GPS Checkup

Keesha was forty-three years old, worked at an office job, and had recently broken up with her long-term boyfriend of three years. Things were not going as well as she thought they would be at her age. She wanted change in her life but struggled with how to go about it, and thus did not believe in herself. When she took this quiz, she scored herself as mostly 2s.

During her self-assessment she was able to identify areas where she wanted to improve, and more specifically, what she wanted her life to look like in the areas of attitudes/mindset, relationships, and personal growth. Her diagnostic check helped her discover what was currently working for her, what needed to change, and what she needed to let go of. She then charted several manageable actions she could begin right away by focusing on her attitude and mindset. Keesha changed her hairstyle, and got two new outfits, but still needed to work on her inner self. These two actions seemingly minor actions, however, were almost like fuel to keep her moving toward what she wanted.

Here's how Keesha responded to her checkup results:

- What surprised me most was . . . *I lacked self-esteem more than I thought.*

- What did I see from the results that I already knew? *I very much want to be in a long-term relationship.*

- What new insight was highlighted for me? *Money and material items are more important to me than I thought. Also, I need some personal growth to become more assertive and outgoing. I discovered that I wasn't fully participating in relationships because of my shyness, and sometimes it created co-dependency in my relationships. I also learned I am very uncomfortable accepting compliments and openly expressing myself to others.*

- What strength(s) did I discover? *I am a very caring and supportive friend, and a good listener.*

- What are some areas for improvement or growth? *I need to feel safer and more trusting in order to communicate more openly and build my confidence and esteem.*

- What one area will I put energy and time into? And why? Confidence. *If I look good and feel better about myself, I will carry myself differently, and I will perform better.*

- Who could I ask for help or support? *My best friend Susie and my hairdresser Frank.*

- What are gifts and talents that I can share with others? *I can listen; be a good friend by being trustworthy, patient, giving and kind. I could be a gym accountability buddy. I always bring my calmness into situations. I'm artistic. And, I am a darned good cook!*

This was Keesha's "You are here" sign: where she was standing right then, in that moment in her life. By completing the diagnostic check, Keesha was able to identify what was currently working in her life, what needed change, and what she could stop doing. Keesha's self-reflection helped her get positioned for success. Without that initial road marker indicating on a map where you are, how can you effectively find your way to your next stop? The same thing happens in life. You can't just call up the local grocery store and say "How do I get there from here?" The store clerk on the other end of the line will ask: "Well, where are you now?" or "Where are you coming from?" or "Which direction are you heading?" We can apply this same analogy to mapping out our future. First, you need to know where you are. Then you can begin the process of getting to where you want to be!

Begin the process of getting to where you want to be!

So now that you know where you are, let's look around and see what may be holding you back from starting your journey and clear any debris off your windshield so you can see the road ahead clearly.

ROAD RULES TO LIVE BY

1. Know where you are right now.
2. Complete your diagnostic check to pinpoint and define your current situation.
3. Brainstorm ideas and options to plan your best life.

MAPPING YOUR WAY

1. How did the GPS Checkpoint Scorecard help you identify where you are right now? Were there any surprises?

2. What did you learn from your diagnostics?

3. What good opportunities may you need to say "no" to so you are ready for great opportunities?

Chapter 2

Clearing Your Windshield and Seeing the Road Ahead

"As you become more clear about who you really are, you'll be better able to decide what is best for you— the first time around."
—Oprah Winfrey

As you set out on a trip, or even to go on a short errand, if your windshield is covered with bugs, dirt, and other debris, not only is it not pleasant to look through, it can also be hazardous. A clean windshield ensures a safe and more focused drive. Unfortunately, without even realizing it, we often travel through life looking through a dirty windshield.

Take a moment to think about the following questions:

- What bugs do you have on your windshield (in your life) that needs to be cleared off?

- What is blocking your vision?

- What are the things (or who are the people) that are blocking your vision?

The bugs and other debris can be the things that irritate you or clutter your life. These can be things that you have started and not completed, things that need to be fixed that you have been avoiding, things you keep saying you'll do but have not yet done. All of these things can create debris on your windshield and make it hard for you to focus on the road ahead.

When you clean your personal windshield, you become more conscious and aware of what's going on in your life, and you can better determine what might be getting in your way and limiting your ability to move forward in a positive direction. By gaining clarity, you will see yourself and others in a different way, and start to see what you need to focus on. An example of cleaning your windshield can be when you de-clutter your home, closet, or office. When you do this, you become more organized, less distracted, and more focused.

Julie's weight was like a roller coaster, she had three different dress sizes in her closet: her fat clothes, her thin clothes, and her clothing she hoped would come back in style. Her closet was full, but 80 percent of what was in there she couldn't wear. In the mornings, it took forever to find something to wear, which really got her down. The beginning of her day was stressful and depressing which in turn colored her outlook for the rest of the day. Finally, she took a Saturday afternoon to take everything out of the closet and sort through it, and keep only what fit her. Julie invited a friend to come over and help which worked incredibly well because her friend was not attached to the articles of clothing. Julie then called a charity to take the items she chose not to keep. The end result was that Julie felt increased confidence because she had clothes she felt good in, her closet was organized, and she could find what she needed in the mornings. People started to notice that she was wearing clothing that flattered her and fit properly. Her increased confidence rippled over into her work.

Even tackling an overwhelming closet job can help clear the windshield. Clearing your windshield isn't as daunting as it might seem. The tasks that you choose don't have to be huge. If something does seem overwhelming, a buddy-system, or sharing the responsibility with someone else will ease the burden and help you stay focused on the task at hand. A buddy system allows you to give support to someone else as well.

Let's look at some of the common things that many women say get in their way and mess up their windshield. Do any of these sound familiar to you?

- clutter
- living in the past
- trying to do too much at once
- no boundaries; can't say "no"
- procrastinating
- starting too many projects and not completing them

As you free yourself from some of the things that may be obscuring your view, pay attention not to use clearing your windshield as an excuse to move forward. You need to acknowledge when it's clean enough to safely get on the road. Focusing too long on cleaning the windshield could be a sign of procrastination. It's like keeping your car in the driveway, always polishing and cleaning, but never taking the car out for a drive. Perfectionists often procrastinate. Because of the need for perfection, they are often clearing and recreating, and in doing so, not taking steps on the journey to move ahead.

Signs you may be a perfectionist or procrastinator:

- You stall on trying new ideas because you think someone else's idea is more thought out and planned.

- You are late getting out the door because you have fixed your hair for the seventh time.

- You cross things off your to do list and put them back on because you believe they need to be done differently.

- You become easily upset when what you planned did not turn out the way you wanted.

- You have a difficult time releasing your work (for example, a report you worked on) because there may be a mistake in it.

- You worry about what others will say about you if you fail or make an error.

The following exercise will help you pinpoint where you may be procrastinating. Look at yourself with open, honest eyes and make yourself aware of where you might be stopping yourself in your tracks is the first step in moving forward.

From Park to Drive

Most of us know what we need to be doing to maintain optimal health; however we don't always follow through. We say we'll go to the gym, but find excuses not to; or we say we'll eat more healthful meals, but still order a pizza for dinner. It's as though there's a gap between getting the car out of the driveway and on the road—a gap between knowing and doing. The park to drive scale is a simple and useful tool for assessing where you are. On it, you plot where you feel you are with respect to items that you feel you are trying to fix, but don't seem be making progress. The scale goes from 1 to 10 where 1 indicates you're in park (knowing) and 10 indicates you're driving down the road (doing).

In Carla's case, she was struggling to keep off ten pounds that kept finding her every time she lost them. She was eating a healthy and well-balanced diet, but was not active enough. She knew with 100 percent certainty that she needed more exercise. She ranked quite low on the Park to Drive scale. (Notice her X is close to Park and far from Drive.)

Park (Knowing) _____x_____ Drive (Doing)
         1   2   3   4   5   6   7   8   9   10

Dina is overwhelmed by the pile of receipts and bills that are accumulating on her desk. She is working two jobs but struggles to make ends meet. She knows she needs to become more organized with her financial management, and get a better understanding of where her money goes. Yet, the pile on the kitchen counter continues to build.

Tanya's job as a counselor is stressful. She knows firsthand the importance of self-care, and in fact recommends to all her clients that they reserve fifteen minutes a day for self-care. She struggles to take her own advice consistently. She is able to accomplish this about 50 percent of the time. She is about a 6 on the Park to Drive scale.

Park(Knowing)_____x_____Drive(Doing)
         1   2   3   4   5   6   7   8   9   10

Identifying the gap between the knowing and doing in your life, creates a higher awareness and forces you to focus. Pinpointing the gaps allows you to take charge, plan, and take action to close the gap. Awareness is a critical component to getting clear on what it is you want in your life.

List 3 things you *know* you ought to be doing to improve one area of your life.

_____

_____

_____

List 3 things you are *doing* to contribute to this area of your life.

_____

_____

_____

TRAFFIC PATTERNS

As you prepare to set off on your GPS best life journey, it's also important to look at the traffic patterns in your life. Going from park to drive is the first step in recognizing areas where you may need to work a bit harder toward change. Looking at your traffic patterns will show you where you've had successes and how to capitalize on them.

There is a tendency for people to always want to start fresh, instead of starting where they are and simply revising what may already be steps in the right direction. It has been said that success leaves clues. Most people don't pay attention to these clues. So what are the traffic patterns, the clues, and how can you identify them?

Examples of traffic patterns are your credit card bill and your bank statement: they give you clues about what you have been up to for the past thirty days. Your credit card bill may summarize how much you spent on different expenditure categories, where you shopped, and also highlight your past spending history. This is one way of looking at patterns. We need to apply this same type of methodology to life. When you look at the patterns that serve you well, and those that cause you to get in your own way, it is then you will move forward more easily.

Brenda had much to celebrate. The employees that worked on her team were embracing her leadership, and the team was finally working together. Morale was up and gossip was down. Brenda thought about her success clues and realized the following traffic pattern: Every time she had success she was in balance, eating well, exercising, not worrying, and focused on her goals. When she thought about the unsuccessful times in her life, she discovered she not goal focused, and seemed to be rushing around, and that nothing seemed to flow. When she used these traffic patterns to success, she was found there was less resistance, and she seemed to get into the groove.

Think about a time in your life when you experienced success. What traffic patterns did it leave? How would you describe how you felt? For example, Brenda said she felt like she could tackle anything and that when she was on her game, she was happy.

- What action did you take?
- How did you know you were on track?
- If you experienced resistance, how did you work through it?

Who did you talk to about your success? Brenda learned she only told those that she knew would support her, be happy and continue to be a champion for her.

It can also be helpful to observe other people's traffic patterns. Take a moment to think about people who you define as successful, or have qualities that you admire. What are the traffic patterns they follow for success?

Joanne shared that she had wanted to meet a specific celebrity speaker. When we asked what it was about this person that attracted her, she responded:

- He is so profound in how he speaks and shares his message.
- I love how deeply honest he is.
- He speaks from his heart.
- It is like he is saying what I want to say.
- It feels like his CDs are speaking only to me.

These are examples of what Joanne could use as traffic patterns for success. By observing and pinpointing these traffic patterns, we can emulate and follow those same patterns ourselves.

CLEAR THE WINDSHIELD

Getting *clear* requires a clean slate, just like the windshield of your vehicle needs to be clean for you to drive safely. The GPS CLEAR method will help you write goals and plans in a way that is specific, time focused, and detailed with actions. Here is what GPS CLEAR stands for:

- ✦ Crystal Clear Focus—When you zero in (almost like looking through a pair of binoculars), it brings focus to and attention on your goal, or actions without other distractions. It is much easier to work toward a goal that is clear instead of ambiguous and fuzzy. Too often, most people spend time, energy, and money on ambiguous goals and don't achieve the success they desire.

- ✦ Logical plan with timelines—Once you know the "what" (your goal), then you determine the "how" (actions and logical plan). The timelines prevent you from procrastination, because set deadlines challenge you to stay in forward momentum.

✦ Evaluated regularly—By regularly checking on your progress and where you are, you can review whether you are on or off course, and make adjustments accordingly instead of after the fact.

✦ Attainable—If your goals are not within reach, you will not have the motivation to sustain your actions and stay in drive. If your goal is unattainable, you will find other distractions to focus on. Making a quick shift adjustment to be more realistic will help you stay on the road to success.

If your goals are not within reach, you will not have the motivation to sustain your actions and stay in drive.

✦ Realistic and recorded— When your goals are realistic and charted, you will see when you are reaching different milestones, and can celebrate your achievements along the way.

As you can see, this GPS CLEAR method is very simple, and when utilized regularly and consistently, it can become a very helpful life skill for all areas of your life.

When you are thinking with absolute clarity, it feels like you have turned your high beam lights on the road ahead of you. You are no longer straining to see the road in front of you. When you are clear, others are clear about how they can help, support and encourage you on your journey.

Clarity helps you:

• quickly identify when you are getting off course

• chart your plan and set goals

• make decisions more readily

• focus on what you want

THE IN-DRIVE MINDSET

Choosing a mindset that is optimistic and hopeful will support you in achieving greater clarity. It is also helpful to spend time with individuals who have a heightened sense of clarity. Clarity and positive outlooks are contagious, just as contagious as negative mindsets and blurred focus. While we mention the importance of being hopeful and optimistic, this isn't to say that you should ignore any negative feelings that arise. These can serve as warning lights or signs that your thoughts and emotions are not on course. The important point is to capitalize on this awareness.

Choosing a mindset that is optimistic and hopeful will support you in achieving greater clarity.

Ask yourself "Why am I feeling this way?" or "Where is this feeling coming from?" or "How is this feeling affecting my mindset and clarity?" or "How does my body react. Is it upset stomach, tightness in the chest, or goose bumps?" Exploring these questions will not only give you insight and clarity so that you can change your mindset, it also helps you move out of the negativity into a more affirming frame of mind. We do have a choice over our thoughts. We can choose what we allow ourselves to focus on and how we react to things. We often hear comments like "That's easier said than done" or "Thoughts choose us, we don't choose them." The reality is, we have more control than we think, and we can turn away from thoughts that are negative, harmful, or that do not serve us well. The challenge is that you have to be aware of what you are actually thinking. Is it truly that you can't or is it that you choose not to? Thoughts are by choice, so you will benefit more when you choose thoughts that serve you well.

KEEP YOUR EYE ON THE ROAD

Every day, make a point to become more aware of the internal dialogue you have with yourself. As you go through your day, stop and ask yourself: "What am I thinking right now?" Catch yourself in the act of thinking. If your thoughts are negative, self-defeating, or unkind, replace them immediately with a positive thought. Try to catch yourself in the act of thinking at least twenty-five times a day, and you will start making this a new and helpful habit in no time. This is an ongoing journey, and takes daily practice. A helpful way to start working on this exercise and reminding yourself to stop and catch yourself thinking, is to post sticky-notes around the house or in your office reminding you to catch your thoughts. These notes will be the visual reminders you need in the beginning to help make this a practice.

ROAD RULES TO LIVE BY

1. Begin your journey with a clean windshield.
2. Tackle incomplete projects. A clean slate sets you up for success!
3. Shift from park (knowing) to drive (doing). Get the car out of the driveway.
4. Identify your traffic patterns.

MAPPING YOUR WAY

1. What do you need to finish so you can start with a clean slate?
2. What have you noticed when you catch yourself thinking?
3. How can you remind yourself to shift your mindset?

Chapter 3

Dreams Are the Fuel That Revs Your Engine

"We are not in a position in which we have nothing to work with. We already have capacities, talents, direction, mission, calling."
—Abraham Maslow

Now that you've checked in with yourself, run your all points diagnostic, cleared your windshield and started to get focused, it's time to think about what is important to you.

What's Your Octane—Priorities

Although dreams are the fuel that will run your engine, as with your car, it's important to use the correct octane fuel for the car to run properly. Your priorities, your values, and the things that are most important to you, are that octane.

People who are clear about their priorities, make decisions based on what is important to them. All too often, however, without even realizing it, our decisions are driven by outside influences. When this happens, it's as though we've turned off the

GPS in the car, despite not knowing the directions to our destination. We end up driving around aimlessly, perhaps seeing some interesting sights, but we only get to our destination if luck and chance are on our side.

People who are clear about their priorities, make decisions based on what is important to them.

Take Danny, a thirty-five-year-old father of two. He has a good paying job in the engineering field, and a healthy marriage. He frequently made financial decisions and big purchases based on what his friends and colleagues had or were buying, not on what he really wanted or needed. He did not need a new car, but when a colleague at work announced he was buying a convertible, Danny himself showed up at work the following week with a new shiny grey convertible. Now, there's certainly nothing wrong with buying material items. In fact, these are important to many of us. What really matters is the reason behind the purchase, whether it's congruent with your values and what you really want. Danny made his decisions by comparing himself to others, and sometimes trying to outdo others, instead of making decisions that were congruent with what was important to him. Danny often regretted his impulse decisions that caused friction in his relationship and financial mismanagement.

Being clear about your priorities and knowing what it is important to you, also helps you to manage your time and energy, and you are less likely to feel torn between priorities (even when everything feels like a priority). We've all had days when we feel like we're at the Indianapolis 500, with people and needs racing past us. The phone rings off the hook, everybody needs something from you now, your e-mail inbox is full, and people are expecting answers yesterday, you still haven't started dinner or that load of laundry. Focusing on only one or two of these tasks will reduce some stress, and allow you to accomplish something instead of having eight tasks partially started. When you make decisions based on what is most important to you, the result is more joy in your life because you are focusing on what you actually want, or perhaps need to do. Taking pride in and accomplishing tasks that involve caring for you family, your pet, or your possessions may not always be fun, but it is necessary. These seemingly small tasks impact your overall goals. This is one great way to live with less (or no) regret.

So, to figure out what your octane is, here are some questions to start with:

- What have I already accomplished?
- What are my strengths?
- How do I view myself?

Maybe you have had a dream of something you want to accomplish that has been nagging you for years, but you have not been willing to chase after it for fear of failing. Your dreams can be about anything, or take you anywhere you wish. Look at the following examples of three very different women, at different stages of their lives:

Fifty-two-year-old Janine had recently lost her husband after twenty years of marriage. She didn't know how or where to begin her new life. She lit up when she talked about being able to have an orchard that she and her husband had always dreamed of. She had thought the dream was over.

Megan, thirty-three, was afraid to transition from working for somebody else to becoming a self-employed business owner. She had been making jewelry as a hobby, and all her family and friends had been buying it. At local craft sales, her jewelry flew off the table.

Sharon, forty-one and a single mom of three, dreamed of finishing college, becoming a nurse, and making enough money to start a charitable foundation to help families in need.

In conversation with Janine, Megan, and Sharon, it took a bit of time for them to pinpoint their dreams. Many people find dreaming and letting their mind wander to different possibilities uncomfortable. Sometimes we're overly influenced by the thoughts and beliefs of others or childhood messages we received: "Be more practical," "Be more realistic," "Your dreams are flighty," "That's impossible." For others, self-doubt, limiting beliefs, and annoying internal chatter start to minimize what they've been dreaming. Negative voices from the past from teachers, a parent, or a coach can paralyze you from believing in your dream. People often back down from trying new things and stepping out of their comfort zone because of someone else's undue influence.

It's important for you to go after your wishes and dreams— your destinations on life's journey. This is called inspired action. Inspired action occurs when you put a plan in place and start acting on it. It's filling the tank in your car with the correct type of fuel. Having a dream, visualizing it, and locking it into your mind, helps you be hopeful and inspires you to take action. Once you've filled the tank, you can enter the address for your destination into your GPS. The destination (your vision or dream) will be fixed in position so you can plot the journey (action steps) between where you are at this moment and the destination you will reach.

Shine Your High Beams on Your Strengths

So often we get caught up in focusing on challenges or things that are wrong instead of on what is right in our lives. Take a few moments to reflect upon the gifts, the strengths, and the talents you bring to the world. Review your personal diagnostics answers for inspiration. Your gifts may be in the form of your personality. Perhaps you have a special talent or skill that you wish to share with others. Maybe it is your ability to make others feel good about themselves or your ability to gently nudge people along when they are stuck. It might be your skill in getting things done or analyzing details before making decisions. Think about the compliments you repeatedly hear from others, as these can also help you understand what your gifts and strengths are.

Eileen's team secretly called her the "battle axe." While she had a somewhat abrasive personality, her strength was in making difficult and unpopular decisions with confidence, and skillfully leading her team through difficult situations and getting the job done. Sadly, people judged her based on her strong personality and not her many skills. Know what your strengths are, you do make a difference. You may not always be told about the difference you make but you contribute to others in many ways.

Far too often we see people expending so much time, money, and energy in trying to improve something that is not their strength or doesn't even need fixing. Focusing on your strengths and building upon those will take you to success faster (and much less painfully).

Ways to Help You "Know" What You Want

Knowing what you want is not as hard as it seems, you just might need a little direction to zero in to that. When you punch in "restaurants" in your GPS, it will display a number of different choices. Then, you must make a decision which one to pick. That decision could be based on your favorite dining experience, what your taste buds are tingling for at the moment, or which one is closest to you. Similarly, when you are determining what you really want, you have to take notice of what you gravitate toward as the road to your destination clears.

Here are a two different ways to explore what you want.

IDLING ENGINE. Set aside fifteen to thirty minutes of quiet time each day. You might be saying to yourself: "Thirty minutes? Do you have any idea what my mornings look like?" Don't use such a defeatist attitude. Have you ever set your alarm clock to get up fifteen minutes earlier than everyone else in the household? You can do this for this exercise. You can complete this exercise in the morning when you awaken or just before your go to bed. Quiet time is like a welcome rest stop during a long drive. Letting your engine idle a bit, gives you time to slow down and reflect. This is an opportunity to clear a cluttered mind of the sometimes overwhelming number of things that we need to do. It is said that we experience and process more than 60,000 thoughts in a day, and most of these are subconscious. You gain a better perspective of your world when you are able to filter the positive thoughts from the self-defeating thoughts. You cannot do this when you are overwhelmed.

Denise, a mother of two small children treasures the thirty minutes she takes completely for herself before everyone else rises for the day. During this time, she does not make lunches for the kids, she doesn't catch up on housework or her grocery list. She takes this time for Denise the person (not Denise the mom, the wife, the Girl Scout leader). This is the time when she can listen to her intuition and inner wisdom and hear the answers to her problems. Without this quiet time, Denise found that life raced past her and she was living moment to moment and crisis to crisis, instead of with a more proactive and focused approach.

By taking time and letting her engine idle, not only does Denise get clear on what is important to her, she is a better mom and wife because she is nurturing herself. Denise also makes time for a ten-minute check-in just before going to bed. This check-in is a reflection of her day: not ruminating over problems and what she didn't accomplish, but more about whether or not she was on track with her priorities, what she learned during the day, and what she was grateful for. The best part for Denise is that when her head hits the pillow, she's out for the count. She sleeps well and doesn't replay things that may have caused her stress during the day.

With all you have to juggle in the course a day, you can quickly run out of gas if you don't take a break to refuel. Taking a break can prevent burn out, reduces stress, and helps you be a little more present.

KEEP A TRAVEL JOURNAL. Some people enjoy the process of writing in a journal. Keep a journal to record your thoughts, feelings, and aspirations. It is amazing how much clarity you experience when you write down what it is you want. Writing things down can make your dreams more real and tangible. Let your thoughts and ideas flow. Do not worry about your spelling and grammar. Just write down your thoughts, feelings, and aspirations. Some people like to start with prayer, meditation, or silence before they get started with their writing. They feel they write with more clarity.

Writing things down can make your dreams more real and tangible. Let your thoughts and ideas flow.

What Jessie likes most about the journaling process is that it helps her clear her thoughts so she is better able to make decisions and determine what is most important to her. From reading her journal, Jessie also notices what may have gotten in her way for her or taken her off course. She is then able to recalculate and get back on track.

Have Car, Will Travel

Record everything that you want to accomplish and experience during your lifetime. Think big, don't let self-limiting beliefs or excuses get in your way. If limiting beliefs or barriers flood your mind, simply acknowledge them and say "Cancel that" or "No thanks" and move quickly back to thinking big. This could take a lot of practice. There will be times when people may think your ideas are crazy and then there will be other times in which you realize you might need to dream bigger. Remember it does not matter what other people think about your dream or vision. Be careful of the dream stealers, people who will make fun of your dream, belittle your dream, or take your dream away. You can sit on the shoulder of the road and watch everyone drive by or you can get in the fast lane because you know what you want and you are taking action to move toward your dream.

Your GPS True Calling and Destination Statements

Having a purpose, a GPS True Calling allows you to live life more fully, to live with intention, and to seek out what gives you joy. A purpose or life calling is like having your entire trip and final destination displayed on your GPS.

So, what is your purpose? This is a big question, and the answer may not come to you immediately. Developing your GPS True Calling statement requires you to stretch (perhaps out of your comfort zone), look out the windshield, and gaze into the future without obstructions and distractions.

What would you do if you knew you could not fail? Would you travel somewhere you have never gone? Would you write a book? Parachute from an airplane? How often do you hear people say "I wish I could do . . . " or "I would love to . . . " or "I wish I had . . . "

Why wait for something catastrophic or life threatening to put us into action?

We know sometimes people's dreams are limited by the lack of funds to pay for their dreams. Imagine that money was no object and you could achieve anything you wanted. The characters played by Jack Nicholson and Morgan Freeman did exactly this in the movie *The Bucket List.* In the movie one of the characters was terminally ill and wrote a list of everything he wanted to do before he died. In the movie he accomplished his bucket list. Why wait for something catastrophic or life threatening to put us into action?

The first step in creating your GPS True Calling statement is thinking big. And then, if you can stand it, think even bigger. The following is a list of questions to get your thinking process started. Ask yourself the questions aloud then jot down your responses. A more enjoyable and effective way to do this is to have someone ask you the question and have that person record the answers. An even more powerful way to complete this exercise is to record your answers and play them back to yourself later.

As you answer the following questions, think about your career path, your financial status, your health and wellness, your personal goals, relationships, recreation, spare time, and your contribution to the world around you. By gaining an understanding of what motivates you, you are better able to add fuel to your tank when you need to the most and keep momentum toward your goal. You may find that even by answering these questions, your excitement builds. This is because you are connecting with what drives you: your true calling.

- What starts your engine (motivates you) each day?
- What makes you want to put the pedal to the metal and get going?
- If you knew nothing could stop you, what would you pursue?
- What puts a bounce in your step?
- What do you dream about but do not dare to do?
- What strength or personal attribute gives you energy?
- What makes your heart soar?
- Think about a time you accomplished a goal, what contributed to your success?
- What would life look like if you had no barriers or limitations?
- When you think of your best life, what (and who) is in it?
- What are you grateful for?

The purpose of these questions is to think big without necessarily having all the answers. They allow you to stretch your thinking of what could be possible if you were to get out of your own way, didn't focus on the "what ifs." Often, it is only after a personal crisis that we are inspired to open up and dream of new possibilities. Life is too short, too unpredictable to not go after what you really want—now.

This beginning work is a huge step in getting a clear vision of your destination. The thoughts and images that are in your mind have an effect on where you focus your energy—hence why it is so important to be aware of your thoughts and to think good, affirming, positive thoughts.

Now that you've completed the above questions, take some time to review your answers. What did you notice in terms of themes in your responses and thinking? Were there any consistencies or recurring information resulting from the questions? Which responses evoked the most emotional connection? What questions caused discomfort or felt more challenging? Do you see a theme developing? Take time to distill your answers so you can create your GPS True Calling statement.

> *Life is too short, too unpredictable to not go after what you really want—now.*

THE GEARING UP EXERCISE

For a GPS to take you to the destination you have in mind, you must enter specific details such as a city, an intersection, the name of a store, or better yet, a specific street address. The more specific you are, the clearer your directions will be. Just like punching in a street address in a GPS, asking gearing up questions brings about answers to what your destination will be. Imagine this exercise much like driving a standard car. You begin in first gear, then move to second, shift into third, and pretty soon you are in overdrive. Each gear shift represents the change to next question, as you see below.

- ✦ First gear: I wish I could . . .

- ✦ Second gear: Why is this important to me? Because . . .

- ✦ Third gear: And why is *that* important to me? Because . . .

- ✦ Fourth gear: And why is *that* important to me? Because . . .

What you write from these gearing up questions will help you focus on your true calling as you dig deeper and deeper to find the essential things that are important to you.

As you think about your winning GPS True Calling statement make sure it is:

- Positive (what you want, not what you don't want, stated in the affirmative)

- Clear (crystal clear and defined with no fuzzy or blurry expectations)

- Within your driving power (choose actions that are within your control, not changes that other people would need to make)

- Shiftable (there is an element of flexibility and can easily be shifted to a high gear)

- Has air bags (your winning destinations have a backup plan and a support system)

As you a zero in on your true calling, you will be able to name your destination. Following are some examples true calling statements and their resultant destination statements including mile markers to reach upon the way.

Sue was recently told by her doctor that she was on the verge of becoming diabetic and had to really take control of her health to avoid health complications in the future.

Sue's GPS True Calling: To live life in optimum health.

Desired Destination: To weigh 140 pounds by January 1.

Actions	Measurement	Timeline	Resources
Join a gym and fitness class	Gym membership Schedule posted on fridge Purchase new workout clothes Attend gym three times weekly	June 1 June 2 June 10 Weekly	YMCA Physician Fitness Instructor
Eat healthy meals	Purchase healthy foods Throw out or give away unhealthy foods from pantry Chart what I eat daily Create a weekly menu	June 2 and ongoing June 5 Daily Every Sunday	Grocery store
Regular medical check ups	Schedule doctor appointment for this and next year	June 30	Physician
Increase water intake	Buy larger water jug that holds 3 cups of water Drink a cup of water following each cup of coffee or tea Drink water with meals before juice or milk	June 2 Daily Daily	

Here's another example of a business related destination that Kristy set for herself after realizing her GPS True Calling. She grew up in a low income neighborhood or as she described, "the bad side of town." Her grade nine teacher had a strong belief in her abilities, and became a mentor for her. As an adult and corporate financial advisor, she wanted to give back to others.

Kristy's GPS True Calling: To live with joy, passion, and peace.

Desired Destination: To start a foundation to raise money for underprivileged families.

Actions	Measurement	Timelines	Resources
Develop an outline for the foundation	Create and document a statement of purpose, values, and objectives Develop a business plan	January 30 February 12	Business plan template from her local chamber of commerce
Name for the foundation	Brainstorm names Develop branding for the name for foundation	February 20 March 15	Contact branding expert Contact communication expert
Market and promote the foundation	Launch foundation Press Release developed/circulated TV and Newspaper coverage	May 1 April 20 and 28	Press release template from Internet Media support

Now it's your turn. What is your GPS True Calling? What is your desired destination?

Just like your car's GPS sits in your vehicle where you can see and hear it, and it displays a visual of where you're headed, it's helpful to write down your GPS True Calling Statement. You may find that posting your True Calling Statement on your bathroom mirror is one way to keep you connected with your statement. But why stop there? You can post your GPS True Calling statement on the fridge or your desk, so it always visible to you. Additionally, you can type your purpose statement into your phone, on an electronic sticky note on your computer, to help keep it in the forefront of your life. You might think, "Wow, that's a bit extreme!" Perhaps it is, but when your True Calling Statement is visible to you and those who love and want to support you, it is a constant reminder. There are many reasons why this is true; however, our favorite five are:

1. Your true calling is the destination your internal GPS
    is taking you to. It will guide your actions, attitudes,

responses, and will steer you in the direction of the goals and outcomes you desire.

2. Your true calling will keep you connected to something bigger than yourself. It will feed you, keep your light bright, so that you can light the pathway for others and help them find their purpose and destination.

3. Your true calling gives more meaning to the trivial or less pleasant tasks in life.We all have tasks that have to be done, but truth be told, we'd rather be doing something different. When these tasks assist you in living your purpose, they take on a different dynamic and value, and are much more enjoyable to complete.

4. Your true calling helps keep you on track, going in the direction you have chosen for your future and your life.

5. Your true calling serves as a benchmark against which you can test decisions.

ROAD RULES TO LIVE BY

1. Be clear about priorities and what is important to you.

2. Determine what fuels your engine, your life.

3. Live your GPS True Calling.

MAPPING YOUR WAY

1. How are you already living your true calling?

2. What fuels you and puts you into over drive?

3. What would setting aside fifteen to thirty minutes of "you time" do for you?

Chapter 4

Mapping Your Plan and Driving to Your Destination

*"Planning is bringing the future into the present
so that you can do something about it now!"*
—Alan Lakein

So, now you have a plan, but you just do not know how to make it happen. Most of us have experienced this at some time or other with New Year's resolutions, for example. Sometimes it is simply a lack of belief in what we can accomplish that blocks the road to success. When you believe in yourself, you invite others to believe in you. Your belief in yourself, your GPS True Calling and destination statements can be contagious. Your spirit can ignite excitement and champion behavior for others, which can go a long way in supporting you in putting your plans in place and into action.

Brainstorm your dreams with others and ask for help along the way. The people you brainstorm with may know the "how" or know of someone they can connect you with. Focus on what you want and the how will often show up. People, in most cases, want to help you succeed. If you are unable to do this exercise with others, you can reflect and ask yourself questions. When you ask open ended questions (who, what where, when, why and how), and drill down, the answers begin to appear and show up. It is difficult to help if they don't know what you need. It can be frightening when you don't know the how's, the how to achieve it steps. What we do know is, there is a way and sometimes we need to trust in ourselves to discover the way.

> *When you believe in yourself, you invite others to believe in you.*

Goals are like dreams with an action plan, timelines, commitment and a timeframe. The key to having a plan (or resolution) that works is having a deadline, a route to follow, and to ignite the commitment level. Resources are what you need to make your action happen.

MAKING PURPOSEFUL DECISIONS THAT ALIGN WITH YOUR GPS TRUE CALLING STATEMENT

Sheila was invited to participate in a community service project in her neighborhood. Her true calling statement was to inspire people to actively engage in their community. She was invited to be on the programming board and welcome committee for her community association. Her internal conversation went like this:

> "Does this community fundraising project fit with my vision and true calling?"
>
> Answer: Yes

"Does this project give me joy, energy and opportunity to
    make a difference in my community?"
Answer: Yes

"Does this community project allow me to fulfill parts of my
    true calling?"

Answer: Absolutely. This opportunity allows me to inspire oth-
    ers, make a difference, and help people live their dreams
    and best life.

Result: Go for it!

As you can see from this example, Sheila used her GPS True
Calling statement as a primary decision making tool. Had she
chosen differently, she might have felt like her decision was not
congruent with her overall goals.

Use these questions to guide you in making purposeful decisions:

- Does this action/decision/etc. fit with my GPS True Call-
    ing?
- Does this project give me joy and energy, and allow me to
    make a difference?
- Does this allow me to fulfill my GPS True Calling?

The purpose of having a true calling is to give you direction,
to help you live your best life, to share your gifts and talents with
the world, and to be your best version of you. When you live
your life focusing on your desired destination, you expand your
energy and start living life with less extra effort.

HITTING THE ROAD

Now that you've set your course for your destination, it's time to start making your way down the road.

The act of driving down the road is akin to setting goals. It is said that only 3 percent of individuals set goals. This 3 percent accounts for the top achievers in the world. You can set goals and become a top achiever, too. When you have a clear picture of how you are going to get there, there is a greater chance that you will succeed.

Kaleigh had a vision of becoming a speaker and author. She had a powerful message to share about overcoming adversity and soaring above all odds, a story that many people could relate to and benefit from. A mom of three children, she shared her dream with her children, and colleagues. She started her journey by setting goals and taking action immediately. One year later she found herself speaking at schools, and not only writing one book, but working on her second. She did this by setting clear goals and developing her plan.

> *When you have a clear picture of how you are going to get there, there is a greater chance that you will succeed.*

Your goals help you map out the life you wish to create and show you how much bigger you can start dreaming. Goals and dreams help you focus your energy on what is important and what you want to achieve. Goals help you choose the direction you would like to go in your life.

Always remember, you are the driver. Don't let someone else drive for you or create your map. Your life is a journey in which you become the person you were meant to be. The direction and choices you make will take you to places you may or may not have imagined.

While Kaleigh's success seemed simple, straightforward, and fast, it was in fact a process. In this chapter there are several tools that will help you achieve your goals and chart your destination. Some of these tools may be new for you, like they were for Kaleigh, and others might be reminders of what you know but are not actively practicing. If you are a visual person, or used to using apps on your iPhone or other technology, you will find that approach here. If you like sticky notes, lists on the fridge, and using your daily planner, you will find those tools helpful as well. Often people use a combination of both. The key is to finding what works best for you.

Your GPS Dashboard

A GPS Dashboard is a vision board where everything in your life laid out in front of you. It's a simple but powerful technique in which you use visual images, photographs, and words to depict what you would like your life to look like or what you would like to accomplish. Now that you've determined your GPS True Calling, you can create a GPS Dashboard that is an overview of what you would like to be, do, and have in your life. You can use the GPS Dashboard for specific, short-term, or one time goals, or for more overall long-term life achievement goals. Images may include vacations, cars, family, material items, your dream home, relationships, and career aspirations. With your GPS Dashboard, you are creating a snapshot of your best life. When you see your future laid out in front of you, it is much like a GPS showing you the map in front of you, then you press enter and move toward your future through intentional action.

The purpose of the GPS Dashboard is to connect you visually and emotionally to your goals and dreams. When you surround yourself with images, words, symbols, and colors that represent your desired future and destination, the images create a stronger sense of connection with the goal and the end result you desire. Our brains easily remember the visual images, which in turn guide us to seek out the resources, people, actions, and tools to make our desired destination become our reality.

With your windshield clear and your desired goal in mind, look for pictures that portray or support your vision. Ensure the images you eventually put on the GPS Dashboard are a complete fit for you. You can flip through magazines and cut out symbols, colors, and images that resonate for you or delight you. Or you can look online for photos, images, or phrases. Don't feel the need to analyze their significance, simply keep flipping through putting aside what resonates for you. Have fun and be open to whatever seems to attract your attention. As you do this process, you will find that you become clearer. Once you are done, take some time to reflect on any themes that may have emerged. What are the images telling you?

No two GPS Dashboards look the same. That is because our goals, our ambitions, and life situations were different each time we created a GPS Dashboard. It is always fun to look back at an earlier GPS Dashboard and see what has changed in our lives, what has been accomplished, and what was perhaps not as important we thought.

Building Your Dashboard

Items and supplies you will need to create your GPS Dashboard:

Magazines

Photographs

Images

Words or phrases

Scissors

Glue sticks

Foam or Bristol board

STEP ONE: GET IT ALL TOGETHER

Search through different magazines or online for images, words, or phrases that represent the vision of what you want to be, do, or have in your life. You may want to choose colorful vibrant images that catch your attention, and ensure that you choose words or phrases that are positive and create an

Focus on what you do want, not what you don't want.

emotional connection. When people do not have an emotional connection to their vision board, they are less likely to achieve their desired destinations or goals. In creating GPS Dashboards, remember to use language that is affirmative (avoid language such as should, could, don't, can't, no, not, will, and want). Instead use present focused and affirmative language (such as I am, choose, deserve, believe, allow, receive, etc.). Focus on what you do want, not what you don't want.

You may even have photographs or computer images that are exactly what you are looking for. Some people like to cut out their own images and place them in their favorite cars or standing beside their famous vacation spot like the leaning tower of Pisa, or a resort on the ocean. You can also do this on your computer with different photo manipulation software. By placing your own picture in the images, you are helping to create the belief that you are living your dreams, and you are living in your creation as if it has already happened. It appears more real and that you can achieve it. All of these images help you navigate toward your best life.

STEP TWO: PLACE THE GRAPHICS

Once you are satisfied and excited about the images, words, and graphics you have selected for your GPS Dashboard, it is now time to place them on your background (Bristol board or foam board). Most people are more satisfied when they create the arrangement first, then glue the images after they are certain of the placement and how the GPS Dashboard looks.

Remember, this collage is more than just a pile of pretty pictures. It is an arrangement of your thoughts and feeling related to what you want in your life. You may arrange them by life category or randomly on your board, however feels right for you.

STEP THREE: GIVE YOUR GPS DASHBOARD A FRONT SEAT

We suggest you give careful consideration to where you will display your GPS Dashboard.

Where will you place your GPS Dashboard? The question may not seem that important at first glance however, for your GPS Dashboard to become a success tool, where you hang it really does matter.

Display your GPS Dashboard in a place where you can see it frequently throughout the day so that you may stay focused on where it is you want to go, what do you what to be, do, and have in your life to be truly fulfilled. Brenda kept hers in the washroom so she could look at her GPS Dashboard while she styled her hair and got ready for the day. You could also take a photo of your dashboard and post it on your computer desktop or on your smartphone.

When you have placed your GPS Dashboard in the best place for you, don't walk past it and say or notice "that's not showed up yet" or "that sure won't ever come true" or "I don't' have that house yet." These are words of doubt, disbelief, and self-sabotage. When you doubt the GPS Dashboard, you begin to attract what you doubt, not what you desire. You lose focus on your desire to achieve. Change the words you say to yourself to words of empowerment and motivation. For example, "I am getting closer every day" or "I am taking action toward my goals" or "Good things are coming my way."

Positive thoughts combined with inspired action accelerate your dream to reality.

Alternatively, you can make use of all the incredible technology we have at our fingertips today. You could use a website like Pinterest to create your GPS Dashboard. If you are comfortable creating on the computer, there are a number of software programs which would allow you to create your GPS Dashboard digitally.

STEP FOUR: PUT THE WHEELS ON THE VISION

Some people wonder why their GPS Dashboard has not attracted the life of their dreams. They think that if they think positive thoughts everything else will follow. Yes, positive thoughts are good, but it takes more than that to create what you desire. Positive thoughts combined with inspired action accelerate your dream to reality. We cannot stress enough how using a visual representation of your dreams in combination with focused action and Getting Positioned for Success will accelerate your journey.

To put the wheels on the dashboard, here are some questions to guide your next steps for action:

- What are my intentions for my GPS Dashboard? How do I see this inspiring action, change, and results for you myself. *My GPS Dashboard will be in my home office so that I can look at this every morning before I start my day. It will keep me focused on my goals, and the actions I need to take to get there.*

- How will I use my GPS Dashboard? *I will look at my dashboard twice daily and pick a specific area I want to focus on for that day. If I choose relationships at work as my focus, I will make sure my interactions and actions are supporting healthy workplace communication and relationships. I will start my day greeting my colleagues in the office.*

- What other tools, resources, and supports might be of use? *I intend to journal every night before going to bed to reflect on the current day and plan for tomorrow. I will note who I interacted with that day, how communication went and how my workplace relationships are changing.*

- What do I need to give my GPS Dashboard some wheels? *Being accountable to myself, and believing in my future. I will print off a quote about teamwork and post it by my computer, to keep this in the forefront of my mind.*

- What does success look like to me? *Workplace relationships feel comfortable, I am included in team activities and project work, and my colleagues greet me sometimes before I greet them.*

- How will you measure success? *My performance appraisal, asking for feedback, and the general feeling and comfort in workplace communications.*

Although a GPS Dashboard can look like a beautiful piece of art, it is not and should not be framed under glass because it will take on more meaning in your life if you see it as a visual of your desired life instead of a nice piece of art. A dashboard is a collage in motion. It can be updated (or you can create a new one) whenever your dreams are fulfilled or you have lost that emotional connection with the images and when you have a new vision. Some people create new dashboards every three, six, or twelve months. Some people prepare them on New Year's Day, outlining their goals and vision for the year ahead.

Visualizing Your Best Life: The Road Ahead

The power of imagination is incredible, and you can use it as a tool to create mental pictures of your dreams, goals, and what success looks like to you. The process of visualization requires you to be still and quiet in your mind, so the pictures can form.

Athletes use visualization to focus on their goals and create a mental image of their best performance. In the movie *The Legend of Bagger Vance,* a golfer so focused on his shot that the crowd watching him actually disappears from his vision until his shot is complete. Athletes limit their distractions and quiet their mind for the task at hand. It is a definitely a skill that you can acquire as well. When you can quiet your mind and turn off the internal chatter, you can focus with intent and determination. Turn your focus toward what you want, just like when your high beams are on while driving down a dark road under a moonless sky. You can take time to focus on your end result by visualizing and using imagery to create your best life.

Imagery allows you to experience part of a story. Imagine someone is telling you a story about sitting on a dock on a breezy, misty day. The mist creates a feeling of moistness on your skin. The dock is firm and supports your body above the water. There are seagulls flying around and calling to one another. The lake has gentle rolling waves that splash upon to the dock. Every now and then the breeze sends sprays of misty water across your face. As you look across the lake you see a rainbow, each color in the spectrum sparkling vividly. From behind the rainbow, the sun pokes through.

You may not be able to create the entire experience in their mind your mind, but you may have felt a sensation of water on your skin, or the firmness of the dock, or the sounds of gently splashing water. The story stimulates your senses; making you feel as if you were a part of the scenery being described. Visualization and imagery are powerful and effective tools that help sharpen our concentration and focus, and at the same time, reduce stress and tension.

Through visualizations we have helped individuals reduce their anxiety and bring them to a state of calmness in which they can improve their health and develop a better perspective on how they can solve issues or concerns that are troubling them. Do you make decisions better when you are calm and can concentrate or when you are stressed and missing out on important facts?

During her nursing career, Debra had patients focus on their breathing pattern by imagining gentle waves of the ocean lapping the shore. The rhythm of the waves coming in and out brought patients to a state of calmness and rest. You can find relaxation CDs that offer sounds of the ocean or a rolling stream for this purpose.

Imagery and visualization have been explained as processes that can help you relax, gain greater focus and clarity, and create what it is you want in your life—your best life. Here are some techniques that will make your visualizing process not only more effective, but more meaningful:

- Choose a place or location that is comfortable, familiar, relaxing, and safe for you.

- Timing is important. Many people enjoy relaxation stories before going to sleep or when in times when they are experiencing increased stress and tension. Do pick a time when you won't have interruptions and distractions.

- Wear comfortable clothing—something that is not too restrictive. Sit or lie down with your eyes open or closed, whatever feels best for you.

- Practice slow and deep breathing: slowly, breathe deeply and then exhale slowly. Try and inhale air right into your abdomen and hold it for three to five seconds before releasing it. You can practice this breathing as you go about your day, driving in the car, waiting for the stop light to turn green.

- Progressive physical relaxation: this involves tightening all your muscles in your body, holding for several seconds, then releasing the tension from the body. Many people choose to start at their feet and work through each major muscle group until they reach their head.

The following is an example of a visualization story. You may find that listening to calming music and focusing on your breathing before starting the visualization story will help you relax and become centered. We suggest you read the story a few times to familiarize yourself with it so that you can eventually walk through it on your own. A couple of other helpful options are to have someone read the story to you or to tape yourself reading the story so that you can play it back to yourself. (Please do not listen to meditations or practice this exercise while driving.)

Visualization Story: Your Best Life

Sit in a comfortable position, breathing in and out slowly. You can choose to keep your eyes open or have them closed. As you breathe, focus on your heart. Feel your heart beating a steady beat, indicating life and vitality. Notice yourself feeling relaxed.

Imagine in your mind that it is three years from today. Picture the date in your head. You are at home in your living room.

You are feeling joyful and excited about the celebration you will be attending in the evening. Take notice of what your living room looks like, of what you see when you look out the windows. Notice and appreciate what the weather is, and smile in silence.

Capture some of the images from your GPS Dashboard. For example, if you identified a new home, where will you be living next year? Picture the home. Is it your current home, or will you be living somewhere different. What is the living room like? The kitchen? Your bedroom? Who lives there with you? What about the property? Is there a yard and if so, what does it look like? Store this "collective" picture into your memory.

Breathing in slowly and exhaling slowly, you enjoy the state of relaxation you are experiencing. As you sit in your living room, watching out the windows, you are reflecting on the last year. Think about your accomplishments, successes, what you have learned, and your growth. What are your successes? What accomplishments have you enjoyed? Who have you served? As you smile, you experience a deep sense of gratitude. Sitting in the moment of gratitude, you also reflect about the people who have shared this journey with you. Think of these people, one by one. Picture their faces. They will all be at the event tonight. You have invited them all.

Your thoughts shift to the night's event: A celebration of you! A celebration of your year and a celebration of what is yet to come!

With gratitude, joy, and anticipation you let your mind drift to what the upcoming year holds in store for you. What will you be doing next year? How will you spend your days? Who will you spend them with? How many days off will you take? Picture the people and activities you are engaged with. Focus on the activities that give you joy.

How will you be growing next year? What will you be learning? Who will you be learning with?

Breathing in deeply and slowly, experience joy with each exhale and gratitude with each inhale. Smile as you breathe. Breathe as you smile.

Imagine that the time has come to get ready for your celebration. What will you be wearing? Who will be going with you? Who will be sharing in this beautiful celebration with you?

As you prepare to leave and go to your event, you turn around and look into your home, and with joy and gratitude you close the door and walk toward the vehicle that awaits. When you pull up to the venue, you notice its beauty. It is well lit, and exudes a feeling of warmth. As you open the door you hear sounds of laughter, heartfelt connections, and stories being exchanged. You are greeted by a receiving line of people who are excited you have arrived. As they shake your hand or hug you, they whisper something special in your ear. Think about what they whisper. As you listen, you feel joy. As you move to your table, all becomes quiet. The lights dim and the spotlight is on you. You are confident. You are focused. You are clear. You are *you!* Everyone is there to support you!

As you smile, you share with them the picture of your best life. In your mind, imagine every detail, listen to every word that you say to the people who have come to celebrate and support you on your best life journey.

When you are ready, open your eyes and take a few moments to write down your thoughts and feelings about your best life.

As you move from vision to action—to driving down the road toward your destination—you need to plot out what will occur between as your vision turns into results. Many of us can create a picture of our best life, but we can also get pretty overwhelmed with what comes next in terms of action steps and priorities.

Even though you see the destination, you'll be less overwhelmed when break the journey up into smaller steps. Whether you like to see the route you're taking when you drive plotted out on a map, or whether you prefer to have the directions written out, there are different ways to break your journey down into smaller distances, as you will see in the exercises that follow.

Your GPS Map

The GPS Map is a mind map, and breaks your journey into small distances and giving you a good sense of direction. It is a visual tool that takes a tradition to-do list to a more detailed task oriented level.

A GPS Map uses colorful pens or markers to capture your attention. Whereas a traditional to-do list is a linear list, a GPS Map uses curved lines to represent your thoughts, but still takes you from point A to point B. Just as all roads are not straight, the use of curved lines helps you connect keywords to what it is you want to accomplish. This also helps you improve your memory as to what tasks you need to do. Our thoughts are not necessarily linear, and this approach captures the flow of ideas.

The GPS Map helps you keep focused on your goals and the tasks you need to do to accomplish them. You will be able to recall part of your GPS Map because of the different colors and their significance. As you reach each journey marker or accomplish each task, you will gain more energy, more enthusiasm, and more fuel to go the distance.

Creating Your Map

To get started creating your map, select a short term goal to work on first. This will help you become familiar with the process and gain momentum as you start accomplishing actions on your list. Often, people are inclined is to set out to accomplish the farthest reaching goal, but then are disappointed in how long it takes to get there. We believe in starting small but dreaming big.

1. Get a blank piece of paper and some colored pens or markers. Draw a circle in the middle of the paper. This circle will represent your steering wheel. Inside this circle, write down the goal you would like to work on. Let's use the example of planning an overseas vacation. You would write "Overseas Trip" in the circle in the middle of the paper.

2. Draw a curved line away from the center and draw another circle at the end of the curved line to a category, keyword, or image that represents things involved in achieving your center goal within your steering wheel. Use a different color pen for each category you work with. In this case, you may have categories such as: destination, vaccinations, passport, appropriate seasonal clothing, airline choice, currency exchange, travel agency or online, house sitter or dog walker, who's going on the trip, budget required, and health and travel insurance. Each of these categories will have a curved line flowing away from the category circle with more keywords or tasks that would be involved in accomplishing the keyword associated with planning the trip.

3. Break down each category and keyword into the things you must do in order to accomplish this task. What if you took the example of choosing the destination and brainstormed what you needed to do with this. You might have branches like: decide what type of trip (adventurous, culinary, cruise, educational tour, tropical, or historic), identify the time of year, talk to others who have been to that location, go to the library or do online research about the area. The other things you might include are: how long you are going for, how much money do you need for the destination chosen, are there any cautions to consider with the destination (health advisory or weather alerts, for example).

Once you get started with mind mapping, your brain starts working like a spark plug, and more ideas flow from each topic. You will start looking at your tasks differently and in greater detail. Because the trip is now clear in your mind, you start to notice things you may not have before this clarity. Ideas will surface for you. You might over hear a conversation with people talking about a recent trip they just took, similar to the one you want to take. You may find your fingers punching in new internet searches, because of the clarity. Just like when you plan a meal for one day of the week, and suddenly find yourself planning for other days, noticing the groceries you might need, and the errands you'll need to run. One idea spurs other ideas or thoughts which lead you to greater clarity. You will soon discover more about what you need to do to complete these tasks. We encourage you to share your mind map and goals with your family and friends. They may contribute to the spokes of your steering wheel and give you ideas for what you need to accomplish your goals so that you can press on the gas and move forward to achieving what you want in your life. By breaking down your goals into smaller tasks and things you must do to move in the right direction at the right time, you are mapping your way to success.

This is how Carla's GPS Mapping went:

Inside the circle she wrote "TRAVEL!"

The lines coming out from the word TRAVEL were:

Documents (Passport, Visa, Immunizations)

Medical (shots, letter from Doctor about medication, health insurance/travel insurance)

Accommodations (hostel bookings, B&B)

Activities (tours, volunteer projects, bus tour, visit family along way)

Item to bring (camera, tripod, batteries, cell phone charger, medication, emergency contact numbers)

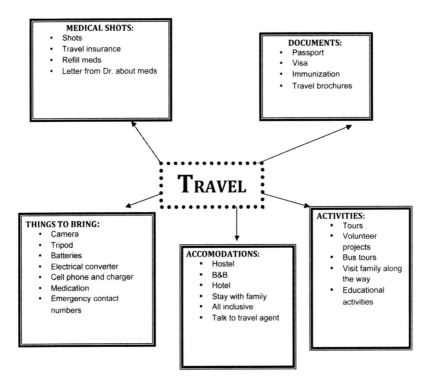

GPS Odometer Tracking

Some people like sticky notes and lists, rather than visual maps. If you are more of list person, you may prefer the Odometer Tracker. The tracker can be used independently or as a support to your GPS Map. If used in support of your GPS Map, it can help you identify the branches in your map, what order to take, and which are the most important actions. The following is an example of GPS Odometer Tracking.

To complete your odometer tracking, identify the tasks or

activities in the left column. In the middle column, record the priority ranking as follows:

A= Urgent/Really Important

B= Very important

C= Important

D= A rainy day project

If there is a deadline, record that date in the right column.

> Here's an example of Beth's GPS Odometer Tracking. Beth created her tracker in with a spreadsheet software and app, and then posted it on her computer desktop and saved a copy on her smartphone. What was most rewarding for Beth was seeing red highlighter every time she crossed something off when it was accomplished.

Task	Priority A=Urgent B=Very Important C= Important D=Rainy day project	Deadline
Review the applications for the Admin. position and forward recommendations to HR	A	Tuesday morning by 9 AM
Call Sally for Parent Advisory Committee meeting dates and put in calendar	B	
30-minute workout or walking	B	Daily
Follow up with John from Strategic Planning Committee	C	Upon his return from vacation

Register Jamie and Sarah for soccer and piano	C	By month end
Schedule quarterly maintenance and tire rotation on van	C	
Measure windows for new blinds in living room and order from Sears	D	
Clean kids closets and toy room and drop off donations to Goodwill	D	

The key to the Odometer Tracking is to complete the activities in order of priority, beginning with highest priority first. May people have a tendency to work through the easy, interesting, or quick tasks first. While it may feel good to complete a number of easy tasks, eventually the higher priority activities can become a crisis when the deadline quickly approaches. In essence, you run the risk of setting yourself up for unnecessary stress.

For example, had Beth worked on the blinds, cleaning the kids' rooms, and the strategic plan follow-up, it would have impacted the hiring and recruitment process for the administrative position, and potentially adversely impacted the company.

YOUR DAILY FIVE GPS

This is one of our favorite tools because it breaks down five things you can do easily, within one day, and you quickly feel success and accomplishment. Like the other tools, this can be used on its own or to support the other tools. The Daily Five GPS will really help break up your goals into manageable tasks, so you don't become overwhelmed or get off track.

The Daily Five GPS refers to the five tasks that you will do each day to get closer to your goals, to help you get positioned for success. These five tasks can be as simple as reading an article, researching something on the Internet, writing a blog posting, sending a thank you card, baking cookies for a bake sale, or making a phone call. Each time you complete one task, you are one step closer to reaching your goal. It is all the little things that you do that end up being big results at the end of the day.

Select one of your goals and think of five things that you can do in a day to get closer to your goal. The five tasks can be related to one goal or even two or three goals that you have chosen to work on. Tonight before you go to bed tonight, write down the five things you will do tomorrow. You will need to do this every evening. Before you know it, you will be celebrating your destination.

Carla's Daily Five GPS as they related to her overall vacation goal looked like this:

1. I will stop by the travel agency and pick up brochures.
2. I will call a friend who has been to one of the places I am considering.
3. I will call the doctor's office or clinic to inquire about vaccinations.
4. I will check the travel brochure or with travel agent about any travel advisories or alerts.
5. I will check with my supervisor to confirm the number of vacation days I can take.

Obviously, planning her trip will involve more than the first five tasks Carla outlined, but the important part was getting started and taking action. The next day, she identified five more Daily GPS actions she could take.

The Daily Five GPS helps you gain much-needed clarity and laser focus. By being pro-active and writing down your daily five

GPS the night before, you will be more prepared and ready to take on your day. With consistent use of the Daily Five GPS, the results you create in your life will be amazing. You will soon realize how much you have accomplished as a result of getting positioned for success. Think of it this way, every week, 7 days x 5 actions, you are 35, yes 35 actions closer to your goal. In one month, that is 140 actions! In one year, that is 1,820 actions. You are miles ahead of those who do not take action.

ROAD RULES TO LIVE BY

1. Map out your vision on the dashboard to create a snapshot of your best life.

2. Visualizing your best life helps you focus with intent and determination.

3. Set up your Daily Five GPS actions. You'll be 1,820 actions a year closer to your best life!

MAPPING YOUR WAY

1. What do you visualize your best life to look like?

2. What is one goal you would like to accomplish over the next three months?

3. What will your Daily Five GPS actions be for tomorrow?

Chapter 5

Release the Brakes

"You block your dream when you allow your fear
to grow bigger than your faith."
—Mary Manin Morrissey

Congratulations, you have learned about all the necessary tools to get on the road and reach your destination. Now, let's look at some of the ways we can avoid hitting the brakes and make sure we keep our feet on the gas pedal.

There are many self-imposed factors that can hold us back from achieving our goals. When we allow things such as fear, self-limiting beliefs, and excuses to overwhelm us, it's like driving through life with our feet constantly on the brakes, slowing our progress, or in some cases stopping us from getting to our destinations entirely.

As you're driving toward your destination, it's important to take an honest look at yourself to see if you're involuntarily pulling the hand brake, or simply not accelerating enough out of fear of traveling too quickly. You certainly don't need to go above the speed limit, but you also don't want to go so slowly that you could cause an accident.

Your mind allows you to see your dreams in action, and can trigger new ideas or inventions. But your mind can also feed you messages that cause you to doubt yourself. Our thoughts affect our feelings and therefore our actions. You can learn to replace old beliefs and thoughts that no longer serve you, with thoughts and beliefs that will support you in living your best life.

KNOWING WHAT RADIO STATION TO LISTEN TO (SELF-LIMITING BELIEFS / INTERNAL CHATTER)

Self-limiting beliefs, worrying, and fear are often part of our internal mental chatter. Think of them as the stations on your car radio: the radio picks up a number of frequencies and you can change stations based on your mood and the type of music or program you want to listen to. Your mind is no different. You can filter the messages that you want or don't want from the internal chatter. You can also stop the internal chatter that you no longer want to hear.

A lot of our internal chatter is like hearing static on the radio instead of your favorite station. The static comes as feedback from our past and doesn't necessarily serve us in our present lives. It manifests as internal nagging, nitpicking, or finding fault. Imagine choosing a different station to listen to, a station that is more positive, upbeat and makes you feel good.

When you notice negative chatter in your head choose to turn it off. One way to do this is to a) acknowledge the chatter (which means you have to be present and in the moment), b) replace the negative chatter with positive thoughts, and c) repeat, repeat, repeat. This process may require you to repeat this step several times. You might say you know it's not so easy to turn off the negative chatter but there are several things that you can do to stop it or minimize it.

Ask yourself the following questions: Is this statement I hear accurate? Do I believe this statement to be accurate and descriptive of my current reality? Why do I believe this statement to be true? Have others told me it's true? What you believe about your thoughts is important. The thoughts that come to your head also influence how you feel about yourself and the others in your life as well.

Excuses Keep the Emergency Brake On

We have all been guilty of making excuses for not keeping commitments to ourselves and others. In fact, sometimes the easiest commitment to break or disregard is the commitment we make to ourselves. Excuses are essentially the little white lies that you tell yourself. Sometimes they are a way of justifying our behavior (to ourselves and others), or to avoid taking responsibility for our own actions. You might say "I'm too busy" or I'm not smart enough", or "You have to be rich to accomplish that." Think about these statements. Are they really true? Are you truly not smart enough, or, can you learn what you need so that you can accomplish what you want to do? Have you actually investigated actually how much money you truly need to accomplish your goals? Are you too busy or simply being unproductive?

Excuses block the options available to you, and your willpower determines just how important your goal is.

For example, you might tell yourself "I cannot exercise because I have small children." There are many ways to fit exercise into your life. You can take your child in a stroller and go out for a walk or you can wait until someone comes home so that you can go for a thirty minute workout. Exercise comes in many forms. Excuses block the options available to you, and your will-power determines just how important your goal is. The excuse of not getting exercise is a matter of how great your will is to achieve your goal.

To help you understand how excuses act like pulling the emergency brake while you're driving, the following questions will help you explore and navigate around the excuses that may be holding you back. You will also explore how to deal with these situations and change what you say to yourself. So, grab a blank piece of paper, and start writing down your thoughts to the following questions. Remember, there are no right or wrong answers. This is simply about self-reflection.

1. What do I want to do that I've been avoiding? What is it I'm tolerating (but in doing so it causes me stress?)

2. What are all the reasons or excuses I'm not taking action toward making my dreams a reality? (Examine whether or not you are a perfectionist, or afraid of succeeding.)

3. What is holding me back or keeping me stuck from moving forward?

Make a list of actions for each of the excuses or reasons that you wrote down. These actions are ideas specific to how you can overcome each excuse you have identified. Excuses can weigh you down and keep you stuck where you are. When you eliminate them from your life you actually stand more confidently in yourself, and among your peers, your family, and friends.

When you identify the excuses that are holding you back, you are better able to understand the next steps that you could take in your journey. As you get rid of excuses, you can then focus on solutions. You can then take control of the wheel and reframe the thoughts that come into your mind. In fact, each time a self-limiting beliefs or excuses enter your mind, ask yourself "what is the opportunity here for me to learn" or "how will this allow me to stretch a little more out of my comfort zone?"

As you reflect upon your answers to these questions, avoid the tendency (if you have it) to be harsh on yourself or to focus on what *hasn't* been accomplished. Instead, shift into a kinder more compassionate conversation with yourself. And, allow yourself to see this as a time of growth.

Connie, who is fifty-three years old and single, loves to paint in her spare time. She always wanted to go on a painting tour overseas but always fell back on the excuse that there was no way she could afford to. She works for government, and felt that this type of trip was far out of reach. She hasn't used her vacation time up, so it would not be a problem to take a month off. When she added up the costs of staying in a hotel for thirty nights, she assumed she could not afford the trip. When she used the GPS Mapping exercise, she discovered that there were other accommodation options, which were a third of the cost. Tuscany in the fall definitely looked like a possibility for Connie.

Blame: It's Not the Other Drivers' Fault

Blame is also an easy rut to fall into. There is a very fine line between expressing disappointment and blaming. For us, the difference is that when you express disappointment, you are assuming responsibility for how you feel. Blame is projecting how you feel on someone else and assigning responsibility to them. Some people like to blame their parents, a bad childhood, or their siblings for their problems. An example that many of us can relate to is being blamed for something that was not in our control or intended. A good example would be a mother walking by her son's room asking him to put the laundry in the hamper, and her son responds "Oh, great! You just made me lose this level on my video game! Can't you see, I am busy?" This is an example of how early these types of blaming responses begin to develop.

Instead of accepting responsibility, individuals often assign blame to, judge, or accuse others. This can result in grudges. When we take responsibility for our part in a situation, resolution is possible and we can find closure to the situation. You have probably met people, who are not ready or willing, to close part of a journey to move forward. When a person acts with responsibility and integrity he or she is more likely to make statements such as, "I'm sorry.

When you learn to accept responsibility, there is far less resistance in life.

I messed up" or, "I apologize. I could have said that better." Or, the person may self-correct, saying, "It was not my intention to hurt you. I am sorry." When this is done, then the toll isn't as great, and a valued relationship can be salvaged, even mended.

When you say something, you own it. Be careful what you want to own. When you learn to accept responsibility, you don't need to justify your actions or be on the defense, or project your resentment or even anger onto others. You simply accept, reflect and move forward. Then, take what you've learned with you so you can avoid a similar mistake in future.

It's important to turn around any blame you may be placing on others and make yourself accountable to yourself, to your goals, and to others. For example if you typically share your frustrations and complaints with individuals who cannot do anything about a problem (for example complain to coworkers about your spouse), instead tell the person who the complaint is about! (More on this in Chapter 6). That is the person who can actually do something and make a difference.

When you dispense with excuses and give up blaming others, you will find yourself empowered. Accepting responsibility allows us accept what is, and to say "that was not the best choice, I have learned and now I move on!"

Sometimes the way you see the problem is actually the problem. Nothing changes until you until you make a change. Take time to notice how you are viewing the problems and opportunities that are presented to you. If you see the situation differently, the result might be different.

Don't Be Scared About Getting a Flat Tire

Much of our negative chatter stems from fear of some sort: fear of success, fear of failure, fear of criticism or embarrassment, fear of rejection, fear of change. It is important to recognize that everyone is afraid of something at one time or another. Some people are afraid of heights, some fear speed, while others are afraid of spiders. Your fears are only as big as you allow them to be. When you focus on your fears, and worry about them, it is like putting a magnifying glass on them. It makes the fear bigger and more pronounced as you put energy and attention on it.

Christina told us that she was afraid of going after her goals for the fear that her relationship would change with her spouse. Her fear of success got in the way of her participating in different activities, and she recounted many times that she experienced regret for putting her fear before her goal. Then she shared her fear about going after her dream with her husband, he was surprised because he saw the potential in her to accomplish her dream. He wanted to support her in any way that he could. When Christina started to put less focus on her fears there seemed to be fewer situations that triggered the fear. "I wonder why there are less things that scare me?" said Christina. "Perhaps because I am overcoming my fears, I am looking at situations differently, or maybe it is because I no longer fear new situations." Sometimes we are afraid of what will happen to our current circumstance, especially if we are quite comfortable or satisfied with our current status of a certain area in our lives.

Sometimes fears can be so intense that they trigger negative and physiological symptoms. We have met people whose fears have been so strong they feel nauseous, have butterflies in their stomach, feel tension in their shoulders or jaws, or suffer from headaches.

We have met individuals who no longer fear the success of their dream coming true because they believe they can achieve it. They feared growth and success and felt their goals were too big. Sometimes the universe or God has dreams for you that are much bigger than you anticipate. When you accept this, you are more likely to attract increased abundance into your life. Darlene shared that the mind mapping exercise had made her dream much bigger than it was before. However, instead of thinking that her dream wasn't possible, she saw all the possibilities open up, and in short order, the bigger dream became her new reality. In conversations with Darlene about

Fear stops us in our tracks and limits our opportunities.

her fear, she realized that her fear had been rooted in seeing her dream as real. She had feared being worthy of her dream. Once she realized what was holding her back, her dream expanded larger and more quickly than she had even dreamed for herself.

View your fears as opportunities to grow and reconfigure your GPS. Part of having figured out your GPS True Calling, was actually a first step in overcoming your fears, doubts, and self-limiting beliefs.

When you understand where your fear is rooted, you can

address the roots, the reasons, and take actions to move through the fear with more confidence and ease. If you are moving through fear, it is supposed to be uncomfortable because you are growing, stretching, acting with courage.

Fixing the Flat: Conquering Fear

Fear is like having a nail in your tire; fear deflates the tire. Like the tire, fears drain our energy. Fear stops us in our tracks and limits our opportunities. The best way to conquer fear is by taking action. It is about taking those little steps toward your goal. Share your fears with others. Enroll them as your support system in helping you succeed. There is a powerful skill that you can use to transform fear and worry into a more positive thought and action, a skill that will put air back in your tire and get you on your way.

Fix your flat tire by following these steps:

Step 1: Identify what is *really* bothering you and pushing your worry/fear gauge.

Step 2: Where does this worry coming from?

Step 3: What do you need to do, be, or have to alleviate this worry?

Step 4: What actions can you take to acquire what you need?

Step 5: What impact will these actions have in alleviating this worry?

Step 6: What will be the outcome if you avoid taking steps to change this thought or avoid taking action?

These steps do three things:

• help you focus on solutions instead of worry and prob-lems,

- allow you to take back control of your thoughts and your journey, and

- help with your approach to things in the future. The more you take action and make decisions, the less there is to worry about.

Instead of worrying about what others will think, use these questions to guide your choices and actions:

- Are my intentions honorable and authentic?

- Can I look at myself in the mirror tomorrow?

- What will I think about myself?

Courage counteracts fear. Having courage does not mean that you do not fear, it means you know how to control or manage your fear. You build strength, courage and resilience when you face your fears and move through them. You may also reframe the context in which you see the fear in a more positive and supporting environment. Always keep in mind that you are the driver and are in control of where you navigate.

The more you take action and make decisions, the less there is to worry about.

There will be times that your goals will be big and you will move swiftly toward them. There will be other times you may move slowly with small increments of progress. What you need to know is that no matter how fast you are going, if you have persistent action, you will eventually get there and achieve your goals. The biggest questions that remain are "What is your will to achieve your goals? How badly do you want to achieve them? What specific action could you take today to get one step closer to your goals?

KEEP YOUR WHEELS ALIGNED

Self-limiting beliefs, excuses, and fear prevent you from staying on the right track and heading in the right direction to live your best life. Having your wheels in alignment is a great metaphor for traveling in a straight line, maintaining focus and momentum in the journey. You will realize that when you eliminate self-limiting beliefs and excuses, you are better able to navigate roadblocks or obstacles that stand in your way. When you are in alignment, your priorities, beliefs, and values keep you true to yourself and on track.

Strategies to stay on track and in alignment:

- Read or listen to inspirational or motivational audio books or videos,
- Surround yourself with positive or like-minded people,
- Make a list of all your strengths,
- Reduce or minimize the exposure you have to negative people. (More on this in chapter 6.)
- Be aware of what energy you may also be projecting out into the world. It you are putting out negative energy in your words or thoughts, you may be attractive like-minded individuals who also share negative words and thoughts.

Words to Eliminate from Your Vocabulary

The words you think and speak are very powerful. So powerful in fact that they can influence your subconscious, not just your conscious mind. The following are words you want to choose to lose! These words can be deflating and can minimize commitment:

- ✦ Never/Always: "You never . . ." or "You always . . ." These generalizations make people feel accused.

- ✦ Can't: "I can't do this!" The words "I can't" reduce your confidence and deflect your responsibility and desire to try.

- ✦ Won't: "I won't make it in time for that appointment!" or "I won't make the deadline." This word results in the same thinking as the word "can't."

- ✦ Should have: "I should have done this instead." "I should have called to say I'd be late." The word "should" often assigns blame to self and others, and feels like a put down.

- ✦ Could Have: "Rats, I could have done it another way." Or "I could have made arrangements." These statements imply self-blame.

- ✦ Just: "I am just the receptionist." This word minimizes your credibility and importance, and therefore devalues you and your contribution.

- ✦ Try: "I'll try and stop by for tea on my way home." This statement does not confirm commitment.

These words challenge your ability to make the right decision, and put the brakes on your forward progress. In order to keep your forward momentum going, use affirming, confirming, and inspiring words or phrases like the following:

- I am
- I'm in the process of
- Or something better . . .
- For sure!
- I can
- I believe
- I desire
- I choose

These words show commitment and belief in yourself. As you start changing the words you use, you will notice that your thoughts will change as well. New ideas and concepts will help fuel your tank and motivate you to travel to new destinations.

Shifting Gears into Helpful Habits

Sometimes it is the smallest shift, done consistently over time, that results in the greatest impact. By doing these shifts, your revenue, relationships and productivity can increase and make the journey to your destination much smoother (and even more enjoyable). It is almost like choosing a better road to take on your mapped out journey.

Determination and commitment are just two of the key ingredients in leading a successful life. You must have the will, the spirit, and the motivation to go after what you want. If you are not motivated to do a task that is required to get what you want, then you probably won't get it. Determination and commitment require effort, which is one thing that cannot be taught. The effort to succeed must come from within you. You must be able to make your choices based on how badly you want to achieve your goals.

Lack of determination and commitment are the brakes that slow most people's journeys. It's something you see often when someone's trying to quit smoking or lose weight. People have a lack of determination and commitment to their goals because they don't see them as a priority or they have trouble visualizing themselves accepting the goal as true. When people are determined and committed to their goals the impossible becomes possible.

One of the best ways to become determined and committed is to shift gears and change your habits. Our behaviors typically default to habits and patterns that have developed over time, yet don't necessarily serve us well.

Famous for multitasking, Charmaine found that at the end of the business day, more often than not, she would find that she had started more tasks than she had completed. She forced herself to change her approach and become more systematic in her business life. She began focus on one task and seeing it through to completion rather than ending the day having started many things without finishing them. This new habit has transformed her business.

> *Your habits need to support you to be congruent with your goals.*

Your habits need to support you to be congruent with your goals. For example, if you want to be healthy, habits of excessive television watching, snacking late at night and limited recreational activities are not congruent with what you seek.

About ninety percent of our typical behaviors are based on habit. Does that surprise you as much as it did us? Think about your day, from the time you open your eyes in the morning until the time your head hits the pillow at night. Much of what you do during the time in between is habit and routine.

Changing behaviors and creating new habits is not always easy, but it certainly is possible! Whether you focus on unlearning or replacing habit, what is most important is clarity about the habit that you want to change. Consider the reasons you want to change it, and begin to develop new beliefs, thoughts, and actions that support the new habit.

How do you know if your habit is unhelpful, or a bad habit? Habits that are not helpful and that are often considered bad habits are typically ones that:

- Cause stress, discomfort, or new challenges
- Get in the way of reaching your goals

- Trigger people to comment or complain about the behavior or habit
- Repeat because it is familiar, not because it is helpful

Sometimes habitual behaviors are learned (from family, through school or role modeling), and other times habits form as a coping mechanism. They are behaviors we have repeated so many times, they are like second nature, something we can do with our eyes closed. These habits and behaviors may be ones affecting your health or your relationships. They can be so ingrained that they are hard to change; however, you know best which habits are serving you and which are not. If you are not sure, ask someone for feedback on some of your habits or behaviors that they like or dislike. Remember to be open to the feedback. This feedback is very valuable in creating your best life. Their feedback is simply their perception, and is not a personal attack.

The following is a list of "bad habits" given to us by our clients:

- Allowing bills and mail to sit unopened and unattended to
- Working too late or working long hours
- Not taking care of the taxes
- Over use of texting
- Texting while driving (Yikes!!!)
- Not taking enough time off work to enjoy life
- Eating too late or not eating healthy
- Drinking too much coffee and not enough water
- Being late for meetings or missing deadlines
- Always rushing

- Interrupting others
- Not remembering people's names after you have been introduced
- Not following through, not keeping commitments
- Making excuses
- Using blame statements
- Leaving things until the last minute
- Not looking after their health
- Smoking
- Not being aware of their finances
- Not letting go of events, regrets, and the past.

If you were to identify a few of your habits that don't serve you well, what would be on your list? There are many different viewpoints on how to change a habit, here's our take on it. The first key in changing any behavior or replacing a habit is to first identify what specifically needs changing or modification. It is also helpful to reflect on why the habit needs to be modified. Changing a habit because you think that's what other people want of you is not a good reason.

Just like a standard vehicle, the grinding of gears can become somewhat annoying, and forces the driver to shift gears more smoothly. Eventually with continued grinding of gears, you can burn your clutch out. The same applies when you shift gears to develop new habits. While changing habits can be a challenge (and make you feel like you are about to stall), and a bit uncomfortable, it is definitely possible to change, and positive changes reduce burn out.

When learning a new habit, pay attention to the internal messages that support you in staying on track. Lock in the coordinates; be very clear on the habits you are changing. New habits take thirty days of consistent practice and action to get ingrained in your life. You must be emotionally charged, wanting to change, and be able to visualize yourself as succeeding at mastering your change of habit. Change occurs when *you* change.

Use the following guidelines as you assess the habits you think you'd like to change:

- Identify the impact of these habits.
- What are you missing out on because of these habits? Are there impacts on other people besides you?
- Take action to change.
- Generate new ideas for action, clear concrete steps.
- What do you need to let go of?
- Look at your belief system and notice where you may need to modify your beliefs (or create new ones) to support you in the behavior change.
- When the old habits creep in, identify them and replace them with the new one.

The following chart gives examples for shifting gears out of bad habits to support your best life journey while getting positioned for success.

First gear (old habit)	Impact of old habit	Habit Replacement	Gear Shift (action for new habit)
Not completing what I start	Too many tasks on the go Clutter and dis-organization Missed dead-lines	Finishing projects and activities before moving to next Organization and de-cluttering	Clean and organize work environment Chart the projects/activi-ties to be completed Identify deadlines for completion for these activities Only say yes when the project can be completed on time Celebrate success when the project/activity is completed
Snacking late at night	Weight gain Indigestion at bed time Poor quality sleep	Not eating after 9 pm Let go of the self-talk that tells me eating late is ok	Stop watching TV as late Snack on healthy foods after 7 pm Buy healthy snack food Chart what I eat and when I eat
Checking email before bedtime	Difficulty falling asleep, doing work late at night, takes time away from my time to read, be with family or meditate.	Keep in touch through Facebook or by phone Use time to write letters Create night-time routine that fosters restful sleep (bath, read, meditate)	Check email at three intervals during the day and never after 8 pm

From the shifting gear exercise, you become more aware of your habits and the actions necessary to move away from the ones that don't serve you, to those that do. This process will also help you overcome obstacles and detours that come in your way.

Changing Lanes

Another approach is to develop skill and comfort with changing lanes by utilizing the skill of reframing a negative or unwanted habit. A great question to ask yourself is: "Is this working for me?" "Is this bringing added value to my life?" If the answer is "no" then change lanes!

Joe works in the trades, has been at the same job for twenty years, counting days to retirement, is anti-management and says "nothing goes right around here" and "I have the worst luck in the world." Joe seems to attract people with similar viewpoints and complaints into his life, the positive people (like his wife) have an extremely difficult time being around Joe in fact one of his colleagues reported "Joe sucks the life right out of me. He's an energy drainer." Joe is not aware of how he is self-sabotaging relationships nor does he believe that an attitude adjustment could serve him well. His supervisors have provided him feedback about how he is being perceived by others, and to Joe, this is one more reason to dislike management instead of reflecting on the feedback and taking it constructively. Joe's behavior changed when his wife had let him know that she could no longer live with his negativity, constant blame and pessimistic attitude. She explained that it drained her. Over time, Joe was able to make enough adjustments and realized that he had more to lose by staying pessimistic than changing his attitude. This was slow process but his wife was willing to provide feedback, and Joe was open to receiving her input about when he needed to shift gears in his attitude or behavior. There was too much to lose if he didn't choose lanes. Changing lanes really boils down to focusing on what you *do* want, not what you *don't* want.

Think of lane changing as a tool to inspire you to achieve your best results. Ultimately, you will lock in the beliefs that keep you on track, support you when you encounter detours, and push you to move beyond the barriers you may encounter. Your perception determines how you respond in life, so choosing positive thoughts will help create more positive responses. We know how hard it can be to remain positive, especially when life is putting roadblocks in your path. But rather than focusing on what is wrong, not going right, or is upsetting you, you may find that putting your energy into what you desire, a solution, or what *is* going right, will help you change course more easily (and less painfully).

ROAD RULES TO LIVE BY

1. Let go of excuses, blaming yourself and others, and complaining.
2. Fears can be conquered one step at a time: take the first step.
3. Align your priorities, beliefs, and values to keep you on track.
4. Watch your words, they shape your actions and create your outcomes.

MAPPING YOUR WAY

1. What are the excuses preventing you from taking action on one of your goals?
2. What is one habit that supports your success? What is one habit that gets in the way and needs replacing?
3. What actions will you take to fix your flat tire?
4. What was one situation you encountered that you were able to reframe into something positive?

Chapter 6

Roadblocks, Detours and Potholes

*"Determination gives you the resolve
to keep going in spite of
the roadblocks that lay before you."*
—Denis Waitley

In order to GPS your best life, you'll need to know how to navigate around the bumps that appear along the journey. The ride is not always a smooth one. You may have found that these bumps often appear just as everything seems to be going great. It just may be that another part of life requires a little more attention.

According to Merriam Webster, a roadblock is something that "blocks progress or prevents the accomplishment of an objective." A detour, on the other hand, is a temporary deviation from your current course. Detours and roadblocks happen in life, there's no way around it.

Along the journey, you may find you need to slow down due to detours, potholes, and roadwork. It is like that for us in our journey. Life will toss you challenges, road blocks and obstacles that will require your attention. Instead of getting frustrated with the challenges you encounter, seek a new perspective and explore if they offer lessons you can learn from.

Sometimes you can anticipate the roadblocks ahead. If so, ask yourself "What could prevent my progress?" Is it that I don't have enough time? Money? Or resources?" Other roadblocks appear due to unforeseen circumstances or when we neglected to pay attention to the warning signs.

> *Life will toss you challenges, road blocks and obstacles that will require your attention.*

Janice was planning on returning to school, but her husband's sudden illness felt like a roadblock. She identified her other roadblocks as: finding childcare, money to fund school and look after household expenses, and feeling guilty for pursuing something for herself when her husband had taken ill. She created a different plan. It did not mean her dream was kyboshed, it was simply delayed. She chose to look after her husband's health and take an online course to get started instead of registering for the whole program. This gave her the flexibility to support her family, while allowing her to take some action on her educational goals. Her guilt dissipated. She felt more secure with her decision because the children were looked after, household expenses were not so much of a worry, and she was able to help her husband on his way back to health. She developed the perspective that the roadblocks can be temporary and can be worked around instead of being a permanent fixture.

HANDLING ROADBLOCKS

When people encounter roadblocks, they often feel frustrated and that they have no energy to move forward because they do not see the options. The possibilities around us are endless. It is how we handle these challenges that determine the success we encounter. Just like your GPS offers you different routes, there is more than one way to get to your destination. You may need to change lanes when addressing the situation so that you will be open to new ideas and experiences. You might plough right through your roadblock or go around it. You may need to ask for someone else's help or guidance. People ultimately want to help you succeed.

Sometimes, as in Christine's case, it helps to see the roadblock as an opportunity instead of an obstacle. She was laid off from her position at work. While this initially came as a shock, and was a crisis in her life, in time, she found she was able to put her other talents and skills to work by becoming an entrepreneur. She enjoyed the newfound freedom and opportunities for creativity. And eventually found that she had no desire to return to her original career. This shift in thinking and lifestyle did not come without adjustments and some financial worry; however, by focusing her efforts and taking action, the situation worked out well.

The roadblock itself might be the fear of making a decision or taking a risk to get what you want but if you carefully calculate your risks and coordinate your GPS you will be well on your way to a new adventure. If for some reason you feel you have made the wrong choice, remember that you are the driver of your life. Make an updated GPS Map. Take control of your steering wheel and head in a new direction; a direction that you are excited about and you are determined to get to.

How you see the world and your own perception of life has a lot to do with just how much you like yourself. When we view ourselves in a positive light, when we genuinely like ourselves, then our perception of life—and others—is brighter and more "user friendly."

Many times, roadblocks appear larger than life. Instead, imagine that *you* are larger than life, larger than the roadblock that you've encountered. Imagine that the problem has been placed in front of you for you to successfully solve it. A strategy to problem solving is first clearly identify what needs to be solved, then brainstorm ten ideas on how to solve the problem, and five positive outcomes that will arise when the problem is solved. Then you can get back in the car and continue your trip. This is how it worked for Christine:

Problem or challenge I need to solve/resolve: Job Loss	
10 ideas on how to solve it	1. Job search 2. Let friends know I'm looking for work 3. Take out a loan 4. Start own business 5. Get a menial job until deciding 6. Move and start fresh 7. Return to school 8. Cash in a savings plan 9. Ask for another position 10. Massive garage sale
5 positive results from solving the problem	1. Reduced financial stress and worry 2. Be own boss- control of decision making 3. Have clarity in a time of crisis 4. Choose new directions 5. Opportunity to plan for next phase in life
The Action I will take (and by when): Develop a business plan within the next month.	

Notice in the preceding chart that some ideas may not have a great outcome, like cashing in a savings or retirement account. However, Christine identified these because they were options. Christine had a small emergency fund to give her a few weeks grace. She decided to put her cooking and baking skills into action and do some catering as a small business. She quickly filled her freezer with pies, cookies, and her special breads for the upcoming farmers market and bazaar.

TRAVELING WITH BACKSEAT DRIVERS

You have probably heard sayings like "you are judged by the people you associate with" or "your results in life are a result of the people you choose to have in your life" or "your life mirrors the people you mostly associate with the most." Sometimes the relationships in our life are not supportive, or healthy, or we remain in them because of obligation or lack of self-worth. It is important to carefully choose the people you associate with. The passengers that come and go in this vehicle called life are there to share wisdom or teach us a lesson. We must pay attention to our internal GPS or our intuition when we feel signals that the passengers are not part of the crowd we should be traveling with. Surround yourself with passengers who encourage and support you.

Have you ever found that there are some people who exhaust you when you spend time with them? Your energy is depleted and your mood takes a turn down misery lane? It's like a back seat driver who is nitpicking, finding fault, and telling you what to do you. Backseat drivers, have the potential to drain your spirit. They drain your passion and spirit by depleting your positive energy. We have to protect ourselves from falling into their negativity by being aware of our energy changes around such people. Just like a positive mood is contagious, so is a bad attitude and negative one.

Often we see people trying to change the energy exhauster's behavior. If you have ever tried to change someone else's behavior, you know this is difficult or even impossible. Remember, it is not up to you to change their behavior. It is certainly acceptable to provide the person with feedback about how their behavior is impacting you, however, time and energy spent on trying to change them may be futile.

Here are some ways that backseat drivers drain your energy, do any of these sound familiar?

- Being intrusive, not respecting your privacy or boundaries.

- Over exaggerating situations. (The backseat driver might make a big deal over an insignificant event or dramatize what has happened. It may feel like the person is trying to suck you in to their drama.)

- Not letting go. They exhaust other people by living in or talking excessively about the past or, constantly bringing up your previous mistakes. They struggle to "let it go!"

- Excessive complaining about others to you. This often puts you in a compromising position. We see this in workplaces where colleagues will complain about one another instead of complaining to the person who is the source of the complaint.

- Criticizing aspects of you. An example is the family member or friend who comes to visit then picks apart how you keep your home, criticizes your parenting abilities, and points out how you could do better.

- Arguing once a decision has been made.

- Making you or others look like the bad guy (blaming others for their results).

- Constantly stressing that they are right, and not respecting or valuing someone's experience or wisdom.

- Thinking their way is the only way (narrow focused).

- Not allowing others to shine.

How do you know if you just had a conversation with a back-seat driver? You will leave feeling empty, sad, disappointed, or discouraged. There is often a misconception that an energy drainer is loud, aggressive and outspoken. This is not necessarily true. Many energy drainers come in the form of a quiet onlooker or the soft spoken martyr. Often because of their own unhappiness, they project this on to others. It is very important to note that often their intent is not always to bring others down or exhaust their energy, in fact, they are not always aware that they do this.

How can you protect yourself from being influenced by the attitude that won't support your GPS journey? Here are some strategies to safeguard yourself:

- Be very conscious of how much time you spend with or devote to these people; limit the time you are with them.

- Be self-aware and fully present so that you are monitoring the impact of their behavior on you (and can see early on when you may need to change the direction of or end a conversation).

- Pay attention to the warning signs your body sends as messages (feelings of discomfort, drifting mind to escape the dialogue, an overpowering feeling to flee or be defensive).

- Be clear and honest about your needs without feeling like you need to provide excuses or rationalize your needs.

- Define and protect your personal space.

- Practice ways to end conversations that you are uncomfortable with.

We can learn so much about ourselves from the behaviors of others. Here is a great exercise to try. When someone's behavior or actions have caused you irritation or frustration, take a look in the mirror. Ask yourself, what is causing me frustration about this? Why is this behavior getting under my skin? Look inward and be very honest. Do you ever exhibit this behavior? The answers you find could be life changing for you!

Then, imagine that you have greater insight about what triggers your frustration, how can you see them differently? Now, look back in the mirror and ask how you can be unshakable, and stay true to your course, and arrive at your destination.

Minding Traffic Signs

The traffic signs we see and obey on the road, are everywhere in life. Obeying traffic signs plays an important role while we drive. The rules keep us safe, keep us from harming others, and help us avoid accidents. The same is true with boundaries. They keep us healthy and promote our level of wellness.

You may find you set different boundaries with different people. For example, it might be appropriate for your friends to call you late in the evening or on weekends; however, you may not provide that same access to your clients or coworkers. This is because you have set a boundary around your time, and access to you. This is a healthy boundary. Imagine if your clients or coworkers had that level of access to you, you would always be working, and there would be no division between your work and your family life.

Do you feel like people don't obey traffic signs around you? People may not be doing this purposely. Consider that perhaps you have not clearly stated your boundaries. If *you* don't set the boundary, people will act according to their own beliefs, standards, and experiences, which are likely different from your own. Overstepping boundaries or not defining them are at the root of many conflicts. Having a discussion to reset the boundaries can be freeing for you, as they provide a much needed definition to certain areas of your relationship. Consider the following:

- What are the boundaries you have established between work and home?
- How do you model these boundaries?
- What boundaries do you have in relationships with friends?
- What about acquaintances?

One way to get a better understanding of your boundaries is to consider information flow. Do you find there is some information you would share with your spouse, but not another family member? If you said yes, this may be a good thing. There should be discussions that are for you and your spouse only.

We've all been in awkward conversations where someone discloses extremely personal information to someone they hardly know. This is an example of poor boundary setting and explains why people get emotionally hurt. Andie was called "the close talker" by her colleagues behind her back. While it annoyed the colleagues that Andie stood so close to them when she talked, none of them had the courage to give her feedback. One day her colleague suggested she stay in her "own bubble of space." Eventually Andie discovered that when she didn't get in people's space, her conversations were more comfortable and effective. Andie's boundaries were different than those of her colleagues.

We teach people how to treat us and they treat us as we allow them to. Setting boundaries, defining the traffic signs and rules we live by, is the way we protect and take care of ourselves. It is important for you to establish traffic signs that honor your commitments and values. Acknowledge and be aware of your energy exhausters. Limit your contact with these individuals, change the subject of conversation, or leave the room whenever their negative energy is drawing you in.

Guideposts for setting up traffic signs:

- Know your priorities. Let others know what your commitments and priorities are.
- Say "No" without feeling guilty. Listen to the requests of others and acknowledge their needs.
- Commend yourself for saying "Yes" to what is important to you right now.
- It is important to recognize your accomplishments. If boundaries have been a challenge and you experienced some success with this, take note and perhaps even chart what you did that worked. That will become a useful tool for future.
- Sometimes you need to be very clear in letting people know what your boundaries are, or your expectations of them. Nobody is a mind reader. The clearer you are in letting people know your boundaries, the less likely they will be to cross them.

Fender Benders

Even if you are the best driver in the world, along the journey you are bound to get into a fender bender or two. Conflict and disagreement are natural elements in life and relationships. Many times, people avoid dealing with conflict or disagreement because doing so is uncomfortable, and they fear the outcome. Avoiding these situations, does not usually help.

When you go on a trip, you typically pack a suitcase with the belongings you will need on your journey. There are people who keep stuffing things into their suitcases, without ever unpacking and getting rid of what they no longer need. Their suitcases are stuffed with their unresolved issues (conflict, emotions, disappointments, and so on). You may be the type of person who has developed a skill for working through these life challenges, and not packing them back in your suitcase. There are others who carry these issues with them in life. These over-packed suitcases are filled with the ammunition that is pulled out in arguments, blame, or other emotional issues. It is important for your emotional health, daily management of stress, and for your successes, that as you work through life challenges, that you let them go. Don't pack them in the suitcase and carry them around. Your emotional health is directly proportional to your physical health.

What are you carrying in your suitcase that doesn't need to come with you? Often people pack their past into their future which creates challenges with opening up, connecting, and living life to the fullest. It is helpful to take a look in the suitcase to check and see what you have packed from the past that is being brought to the future.

Resolving life issues requires you to develop skill and ease in working through disagreements and conflicts. The model we share with you will serve like your road map or instruction guide for addressing life's conflicts.

To address disagreement and conflict, you must get positioned for success by having an attitude of resolution or hope. This means you create a hopeful mindset, paying attention to the internal (and external) language you are using, and the signals you are giving off. The mindset you have will enter the conversation with you, and likely impact how you speak to the other person.

Suzie was extremely uncomfortable with conflict. So uncomfortable that the very thought of disagreement caused her heartburn and butterflies in her stomach. She expended a lot of energy avoiding disagreement to keep the peace. When disagreement occurred with her mother, she experienced these physiological responses in super-size capacity. Her thoughts took her through the following internal chatter:

"Oh no, not again."

"I can't go through this again."

"I am sure she'll just disregard me and monopolize, just like she always does."

"Ugh, I feel sick to my stomach just thinking about this."

"I need this like I need a hole in my head today."

"This is one conversation I sure don't need today."

"I am absolutely dreading this conversation!"

Her internal chatter was plagued with despair, fear, and avoidance. It was not surprising that whenever she had a conversation with her mother, these thoughts and this mindset directed her behavior. In conflict situations, Suzie would sink into the furniture, hold her head low, and use powerless language. In response, her mother's emotions flared because she felt Suzie was uninterested, aloof, and not committed to the conversation.

In conflict resolution, both Suzie and her mother had a huge *aha* moment. They had each been making quite a few assumptions about each other and discovered that about 90 percent of these assumptions were inaccurate. Each was misreading the other's verbal and non-verbal communication, which resulted in their conversations hitting bumps and going off track. The lesson here is to enter the dialogue with affirming thoughts and mindsets such as:

"I can do this."

"I am skilled at having a respectful, mutual dialogue with my mother."

"We can get through this."

ROADMAP TO RESOLUTION

Here is the roadmap to setting up a conversation that will result in a positive outcome, rather than the stress and negativity that comes from conflict:

STEP 1: GETTING READY Preparing paves the way for success. Paving the way involves tasks such as:

- Freeing yourself of assumptions
- Creating a new mindset
- Choosing your words in advance
- Picking the right time and the right place for the conversation
- Leaving your suitcase at the door
- Jotting your thoughts down on paper
- Rehearsing your part of the conversation (doing this in front of a mirror is very helpful)

Getting ready paves the way to success.

Getting ready may also involve activities such as reflecting on the strengths of the relationship, or times in the past when conflict has been addressed in a successful manner.

Questions to consider in getting ready and prepared:

- What assumptions have I made?
- What assumptions do I think the other individual may have made?
- How are these assumptions impacting us or the situation?
- Where would be the best time and place to have our conversation?
- What can I say that will set the stage for a positive conversation?

STEP 2: PINPOINTING THE ISSUE(S) Although this is the pivotal part of addressing the disagreement or conflict, it is also the point where many conversations go off the tracks. Sometimes this happens because both you and the other person might have a different idea of what the issue is. If the issue is not clarified, the conversation will be more difficult and most likely to derail. Inevitably as people begin to identify the issue, there is a degree of storytelling that occurs. It is important to keep the story telling to a minimum, until you identify the issue(s) to be resolved or discussed. Think of this as setting a framework for the agenda. It is a point of reference to keep the conversation focused, and collaborative. An issue can be named with three words or less.

Consider not only the words you will choose, but your intent behind them, and how others will perceive what you have said. This piece of advice would serve you well in any conversation. Sometimes the hardest part of the conversation is "where do we begin." Here are some questions that might help:

- What is/are the issues?
- What question can I ask the other person to see what he/she thinks the issue is?

STEP 3: TWO-WAY COMMUNICATION A successful conversation benchmark is not so much about what you said as it is about how well you were understood by the other person. Mindfulness is about being aware, insightful, and in tune with others—and, of course, yourself. When you practice mindfulness, things shift because your negative thoughts, beliefs, judgments, and assumptions are released. Additionally, emotions are more in check which means you respond better to others.

Two way communication is the most difficult (and in some cases painful) part of the conversation, but likely the most important. Each person shares their perspective, their interests, and needs. As the discussion unfolds, use attentive listening. What you learn by be invaluable. Understanding each person's perspectives is the outcome.

> *We can't solve the past. But, the present can be dealt with, and so doing helps predict future outcome.*

Both you and the other person have an important perspective to communicate. Speaking from your heart allows communication to be more heartfelt. This in turn, creates better connections which facilitates that a better flow of "back and forth" can be both stated and received. Asking questions and being curious is a good way to avoid becoming judgmental or defensive in the conversation.

We can't solve the past, but the present can be dealt with, which absolutely helps predict the outcome of the future. Persevere through the fear! Avoid the temptation to compromise too early, sometimes with a little more discussion and additional information, you will find additional alternatives become apparent and compromise may not be the best solution. Here are questions to consider:

- What do I need to say that might be difficult?
- How can I frame it so it is easier to hear?
- What might I need to hear that will be difficult to hear?
- What are my interests, what is driving my position?
- What are my needs? My fears?

STEP 4: EVALUATING YOUR ROUTE The dialogue may reach a point where you and the other individual both feel understood and that the conversation naturally moves to a discussion of options, possible next steps, or a mutual willingness to move to closure. You may feel as if a shift has occurred, something feels different in the relationship. This may well be the moment of transformation.

As options begin to surface, you may want to jot them down, take note, or summarize the options that exist or were discussed in your conversation.

Together, you will choose a solution that will work best for you, one that you can champion, live with, and commit to. Agreement is not essential, in fact, sometimes mutual understanding and being heard is all that was required.

STEP 5: OUTCOME This is where the rubber meets the road, the solution. From your options, an outcome may be chosen and agreed upon by you and the other person. Often the increased understanding leads to a solution that not only addresses or resolves the conflict but enhances the communication and relationship. In other cases, it is purely the enhanced understanding, perspective changes, or learning that has brought the issue to closure, and no specific solution or outcome is necessary. When disagreements and conflicts are resolved, it is important to acknowledge the work you both did, and your success. This gets you both back on track for future successful conversations.

When disagreements and conflicts have been discussed, and resolved it means we need to let go. While not always easy, letting go allows you to move forward. The challenge is that you may be prepared to let go, but the other person is hanging on to the old, the past or his/her own "stuff" in the suitcase. Letting go means that new "stuff" is not being added to the suitcase and carried forward into the future. Letting go allows you to begin with a clear path ahead of you.

DETOURS: ASK FOR DIRECTIONS

Sometimes you may need to stop and ask for directions from others who have been where we want to go. Some people may tell you that asking for directions is a sign of weakness. We see this quite the opposite; in fact, asking for directions is a sign of strength. You know that asking for directions will ensure that you're on the right path. The definition of sense of direction is "a general conscious awareness" or "an awareness of your orientation in space."

Do you ever notice when you are lost, you begin to feel anxious or uncomfortable because you do not know where you are. But keep in mind that if you lose your way, you can always turn around or start fresh and head in a new direction. The possibilities are limitless. There are rest stops along the way, good friends, social groups, meditation and prayer, mentors or coaches, and mastermind groups who can help you along your route and accelerate your success. Following are just some of the ways that you can press the gas and accelerate along the life's journey.

What holds you back from asking for direction? Is it the fear of rejection? Is it the fear to ask for what you want? Asking for what you want does not have to be difficult. Having the courage to ask and creating a win-win with the person, heightens your chances of success. You may find it helpful to ask with confidence and conviction expecting to get a "yes." What two things would need to happen to increase your confidence when asking for directions?

What is one thing you can do in the next three days to practice this skill? Following are strategies you can use when you ask for directions:

- Practice asking for smaller things before you go for the big one to build up your confidence.
- Be clear about what it is you want.
- Believe you deserve to have what you ask for.
- Review objections; think about the reasons the person you are asking may say no.
- Prepare; know your information. The person you are asking may want more information. Develop responses to possible objections. Again they may need clarification or more information.
- Visualize hearing YES!
- Create a Win-Win situation. What might the person need from you? You might not always know but can think about some possibilities.
- Acknowledge the person's skill or talent when asking.
- Appreciate their time.
- Be grateful for the lesson. The more times you ask, the better you will become at asking.

Have you ever asked your employer for time off to go on vacation and been denied? How many of us would have just walked away without asking again? It has been our experience that sometimes you need more than once, more than twice, and sometimes even three times before the person you are asking might say yes. When you ask for what you want and don't receive it right away, think about how you could make change your question for the better for both parties? Many people ask just ask assuming that the answer will be no. What they fail to do is, is to ask with the determination and commitment of how important what they are asking for is for them and the willingness to create a win-win situation that everyone can celebrate. By going in with the mindset of believing that you will get what you want and creating a win-win situation for everyone involved, you can ask for what you really want and be grateful.

Asking may also include asking for help. Help may come in different forms—support, feedback, resources, assistance, etc. We have all struggled through a situation far longer than perhaps we needed to. We have found that typically people want to help. Sometimes they just don't know how they can be of help. So you need to let others know.

Be clear on what it is you want and need, so that others know how to help you. Time and time again people will ask for something they need or want but are not clear about it. They become frustrated that no one is helping or supporting, but it may because they don't know *how* to help or support you. When you are clear, others can see more clearly what you want. You need to know who you should ask, what you should ask, and how long it might take you to get there. To get better answers, you may need to ask better questions.

Road Rules to Live By

1. Navigate your roadblock and obstacles with consistent effort.

2. Don't give the wheel to the backseat drivers.

3. Don't pack your past into the future.

4. Resolve fender benders as soon as possible.

Mapping Your Way

1. Who are the back seat drivers in your life?

2. What is a conflict or disagreement that you could have handled differently?

3. What have you been carrying in your suitcase that you now need to let go of?

Chapter 7

Staying on Track and Recalculating Your GPS

"Motivation is what gets you started.
Habit is what keeps you going."
—Jim Rohn

Look how far you have come on this journey, working through the exercises and getting positioned for success—your own GPS. When you first started you needed to gain clarity and now you have a clear plan, sense of direction, a map to get there, tools to help you move forward without hitting the brakes, and tools to overcome roadblocks. You're picking up speed and adjusting behaviors and habits to support your success.

Part of staying on track is to review your daily accomplishments. When you review your accomplishments, progress, and achievements on a daily basis, you will likely find that your enthusiasm soars, and that you can correct areas that need improvement as they appear. The daily review inspires you to keep going, and realize that you are miles closer to where you want to be.

In essence, this process allows you to readjust your routine, and recalculate your road map as needed. Reviewing your daily accomplishments can be as simple as the following chart where you can list and rank your daily activities:

Daily Tasks	1	2	3	Comments
De-clutter office		X		Just clean out desk drawers
Take 30-minute walk	X			

You can use the ranking scale:

1= Completed

2= So close

3= More to be done

CHECKING YOUR REARVIEW MIRROR

You may have heard the phrase that hindsight is 20/20. Checking your rearview mirror, self-reflection, is about having a greater awareness about who you are and where you are going, as well as what has worked and what needs a tune up. Each success is built on the experiences you had before the success. Self-reflection helps you keep this front of mind and on track moving toward your goal. Take a moment to write down a recent event from the past six months that may not have gone the way you had anticipated. Ask yourself the following questions or write down your responses.

- What in this situation went well?
- What would I do differently the next time I encounter this situation?
- What lesson did I learn from this situation?

It is only when we take time to reflect about what we've learned that we truly begin to grow into our highest potential. Reviewing these questions and your answers, can you see now some areas where you could have asked (e. g. for help, advice, time, or resources). This type of self-reflection is so powerful in changing your future.

Other forms of self-reflection might include meditation and prayer which help develop trust, faith, and belief in your abilities. When you focus on knowing that there is a source or a higher power, whatever that higher source is for you, you develop a sense of security in the belief that no matter what happens in your life you will have all the tools to get through any challenges that come your way. Prayer is a powerful tool in which you ask for help, praise God, or show gratitude for the gifts you have received. Meditation allows God to speak to you as you focus on clearing your mind. Some people may pray and others mediate. Others may use both to establish a connection with God.

You have been given a free will to make choices that will put you in drive or in reverse depending on the choices you make. When you take time to be still, stop, and sit in silence, you will be better able to make your choices. In Dr. Wayne Dyer's book, *Getting in the Gap,* he states that people practice meditation for many reasons such as improving clarity of vision, finding more peace, and improving healing and memory. He explains the gap as pauses of silence between words in prayers and having a conscious connection with God. As you meditate or pray, you will feel more confident with your choices knowing that you can take on any situation as you move forward to your destination.

Checking for Blind Spots

Blind spots can be the aspects of ourselves that are hidden or suppressed, but that others readily see. One surefire way to deal with blind spots is to ask others for feedback.

Eileen was a lovely lady, very bright and personable; however, her non-verbal expressions were so demonstrative that often she appeared stern and even angry. When others noticed the expressions and inquired about this by checking in if everything was OK, because her face was very angry looking, Eileen was horrified. She stated that she was in a fantastic mood; the feedback helped Eileen understand that sometimes her intensity and facial expressions came across the wrong way to her colleagues and clients. Dealing with blind spots requires courage. In Eileen's case, the colleagues needed courage to provide her with feedback. Eileen required courage to be able to a) accept the feedback, and b) respond and make necessary changes.

Blind Spot Exercise

Write down the areas in your life where people have given you feedback, as they may be pointing out your blind spots. What are the blind spots in your life that you can change? When you acknowledge the blind spot you can move forward or find someone who can assist you in some way.

- What kind of person do you need help you develop that particular blind spot area?
- Is it someone you already know?
- Have you asked anyone for help?
- What feedback would you like to have that you haven't asked for yet?

Pacing Your Journey and Filling the Gas Tank

Just as with any road trip, you need to make sure you make the most of the hours you're on the road and pay attention that you don't run out of gas.

How much time would you say you spend each day on unimportant things; tasks and activities that don't really contribute to your success or to reaching your goals? Do you really *know* how much time you spend reading junk mail, tidying the house, running errands, talking to friends or colleagues, responding to emails, or hanging out on Facebook?

Most of us have thought or said "If only there were more hours in the day. I could get so much more done I just had another half hour each day." Most of us don't have a clear idea of where and how our time is actually spent. We also find that throughout the day, we function at different levels of motivation and effectiveness as our energy and interest levels fluctuate. Your effectiveness and interest is affected by the amount of sugar in your blood, how long you have been sitting, routine distractions, stress (physical and emotional), just to name a few.

A Mileage Log will help you to understand how you actually spend your time. The first time you use a Mileage Log you may be surprised, startled, or even concerned to see the amount of time that you may have wasted. Try keeping a Mileage Log for a seven-day stretch. At first it might seem tedious and you may even forget to track your mileage. Be patient with the process because the results could be extremely valuable showing you where you are wasting time, where you can streamline, and where you can make better use of your time and energy. Some people like to print this sheet; others like to use their notepad on their smartphone or their calendar. Use whichever method you are more likely to be consistent. Here's an example of Anna's morning routine. Once she filled out her mileage log, she realized how much time she actually wasted on the computer and was able to plan more effective use of her time.

Mileage Log

Time From___ to____	Activity or Task	Duration (minutes)	Importance High, Med., Low	Comment
6–6:30 a.m.	Exercise	30 min	High	
6:30–7:00 a.m.	Checked Facebook	30 min	Low	Use time better. Check e-mails and plan for the day while I have breakfast. This would open up a time for meditation.
7:00–7:15	Planned the day and set priorities	15 min	High	
7:15–7:30	Breakfast and check e-mails	15 min	High	Could probably combine the time
7:30–8:15	Got ready for work	45 min	High	45 minutes? I know I can get ready in less time than that.
8:15–8:45	Drove to work	30 min.	High	If I manage my time better in the morning, I can get to work on time. I can use my driving to listen to a motivational CD.

What does your Mileage Log tell you about yourself? About how you manage your time and where your time actually goes in a day? As you review your log, where are you wasting time? Where you could gain a few more minutes in the day? Here are some strategies to help you gain more time and reduce wasted time:

- Look where your energy and focus is required least and explore delegation. For example, maybe it is time to get the kids to learn how to do laundry.

- Planning meals for a few days at a time and do shopping once.

- Check e-mail at certain intervals not all the time. Give yourself a certain amount of how time to surf the Internet or click around on social networking sites. Set a timer to remind yourself it's time to move on more important matters.

- Keep a calendar of when to pay bills, and keep them all in one place so you don't have to go searching for them.

- Keep the kids sporting gear together in one place so you avoid the mad rush of trying to find the equipment when it's time to go to the game.

- Have a binder with a tab for all family members and their activities, and keep papers and calendars there.

- Mark important dates on calendars.

- Have a stack of greeting cards, thank you cards, and gift wrap in your car for those last minute gifts and a stack of cards at home (so you don't have to make multiple trips to the store).

- Look where your energy and focus is most required and attend to those items first.

Next week, implement a few of these actions, redo the chart, and see if you have been able to free up some time. What's working for you?

REEVALUATE THE ROUTE

Another strategy for staying on track is that of reevaluating your route. You can do so after a project or goal has come to completion. There are three questions that guide you in effective reevaluating the route. By charting responses to these three powerful questions, you identify learning that can help you in the present and in the future. Often this learning can save you heartache, time, and resources.

Use these questions to learn from the milestones, and completed actions along your journey.

Date:	
What worked well?	
What could have been different?	
What recommendations or ideas did I learn to use next time?	
Notes to myself:	

How can you use this process to help you change behaviors and move steadily on toward your destination?

For example, Linda evaluated her route to reflect on her recent move. She reported that nothing was broken or lost; moving over a period of time (several weekends) allowed her the time to paint the new home before completely moving in.

She thoroughly enjoyed the de-cluttering process that saved from packing items she no longer needed. She learned that she was more of a pack rack than she thought. She discovered that she spent way too much money on boxes and plastic storage totes that she'll never use again; she underestimated how long it would take to pack, and did not plan for household items she would need that had already been moved to the new home.

How can you use this approach to live your best life? Readjustment may involve traveling a different route. There is nothing wrong with this, especially if it will work better than the route you were on.

LIFELONG DRIVER'S ED

Imagine going through life and not learning something new for a year. Not learning anything about yourself or another person; not trying a new recipe or implementing a new skill. What would life be like? If you said boring, unfulfilling, and incomplete, you are right. Learning and growing are gifts that life provides us. When you are open to learning and growing on your journey, you will discover things about yourself that would have otherwise remained a mystery.

Education does not have to cost a lot of money. It does not have to consume a lot of your time. We have found ways to maximize our time and our learning. By listening to self-help programs, motivational CDs, and educational audio books while you drive, you are maximizing your learning without spending extra time doing this. We refer to this as "Automobile University," a saying used by other experts in the field of self-development. Adding 15 minutes of audio learning while you're driving or exercising can turn into 65 hours of learning in a year. And we gave you the weekends off in this calculation. Imagine how many pleasure or professional development books you could listen to in 65 hours! If you implement one thing from every quarter hour of learning that would be 260—they could be part of the daily 5 GPS or something additional. This could bring about huge change and results!

You can borrow audio learning CDs from the library, or e-books for your e-reader. Better yet, create a learning circle with your friends and colleagues. Exchange CDs and programs and every month and meet for coffee to share your learning with one another. We learn a great deal through teaching and supporting others. Strength comes in numbers so associating with others who are on a similar journey will contribute to each of you being more successful!

INTUITION

Intuition is a big part of staying on track, keeping your motivation high, and retaining that degree of clarity. Our colleague, Irene Martina, speaker, author, clairvoyant, and expert on dream analysis told us that "On the road of your life, your intuition should be your steering wheel, not your spare tire!"

She further explained that your intuition is very powerful and is a deep sense of knowing, and much like your internal GPS system, it will guide you and keep you on track or on the TRAIL Irene explains the TRAIL as:

T—Trust your intuition

R—Relax into it

A—Awareness; you must be aware to listen to your intuition

I—Imagination

L—Listen to your intuition

STAYING ON TRACK AND RECALCULATING YOUR GPS   115

What a fabulous model to help us stay on our journey, and to avoid unnecessary challenges that may arise. Your intuition can save you time, grief, and money if you listen to it.

When you follow your intuition, you gain energy, power, and spiritual connectedness, and this, says Irene, is the benefit of your attentiveness and acceptance of your intuition. We all know what it is like when we don't trust our intuition, we have all disregarded it or argued it. Think about a time when your inner voice said "Turn here" and you chose a different route. That different route was slower or perhaps you got lost. Usually when you don't listen to your intuition, you later say "Geeze, I knew I should have turned the other way!"

There are a number of ways to turn on your intuition and stay on track:

- ✦ Trust and listen to your intuition. Avoid the urge to argue it, dismiss it, question it, or minimize it (or over analyze it). These reactions are fear-based, and when you learn to trust your intuition, you trust yourself. If you struggle with perfectionist tendencies, this will be hard as it requires you to release some of your need for control. When you do, and become more comfortable, you will learn to trust yourself more, and see the benefits.

- ✦ Check the intuition "on" switch throughout the day. Ask yourself "How do I feel" and other questions that ensure you are in a state of awareness.

- ✦ Pay attention to the signs. When you drive your vehicle, you pay attention to signs and trust them, we must do the same with the signs that we receive from our intuition.

- ✦ Reward and recognize. When you connect with your intuition reward and recognize yourself. It will encourage you to continue listening to your intuition.

✦ Navigate through the fog. Intuition is not always clear and does not always provide crystal clear signs and messages. Learn to become comfortable with what is unclear and ask questions to remove the fog.

✦ Manage the fear. Intuition does not work very well with fear. We are all born with intuition; some of us just have not turned on the switch. When you manage your fear, you are more open to receiving messages and accepting your intuition. Sometimes our upbringing has imposed negative connotations related to intuition. Working through these blocks will help you remain open.

KEEP YOUR BATTERY CHARGED

To stay on track, it's important to keep your motivation high and your battery charged. Here are some things to consider:

- Schedule free time just for you.
- Have a great ideas book, keep track of all the ideas that you have.
- Post and say your GPS True Calling and/or destination statement aloud, every day (even several times each day).
- Create an applause file, wins log, or inspiration file (keep thank you notes, warm-fuzzies that people give you and read them when you are having a less than joyful day or when feeling off course).
- Start earlier—don't wait until the last minute.
- Contribute to the community.
- Create more variety in your life.
- Have intentional down time, planned breaks.
- Perform acts of kindness.

ROAD RULES TO LIVE BY

1. Stay on track with a daily review of accomplishments and areas that need improvement.

2. Ask for feedback to deal with your blind spots.

3. Commit to lifelong driver's education.

MAPPING YOUR WAY

1. How has your intuition served you?

2. What do you do to keep your batteries charged?

3. In reviewing your mileage log, where have you lost some of your time? How can you better plan your mileage for the day?

Chapter 8

You Are There! Now What?

"The road leading to a goal does not separate you from the destination; it is essentially a part of it."
—Charles DeLint

So you've arrived. It was so exhilarating to pull up to your destination after all your efforts, getting clear, mapping the plan, dealing with roadblocks and detours, and staying on track. We see examples of this every two years as we watch the Olympics and see many of the athletes reach their destination after many long hours of preparation, training, and hard work; they have finally arrived at their destination. The journey of getting to the Olympics may not have been as smooth as a well-paved highway. The athletes did not get there after a day or two of training but after countless hours of dedication, courage, strength, and hard work.

We all arrive at our destination at different times in our lives, as our mileage indicates on the odometer of our dashboards. Each goal is achieved at a different time. It is important to acknowledge when your goal is achieved before you set new goals. They will motivate you to continue your journey and live to your highest potential.

When you reach your destination, it may mean a new journey begins. How exciting! Here are a few strategies to support you when you reach a destination.

- Know when you have arrived.
- Learn from the journey.
- Thank or acknowledge those who came on the journey with you or that you met along the way.
- Create new goals, update your GPS Dashboard, ensure your true calling and destination statements are still relevant and current.
- Track your success in your wins or success file.
- Seek ways to share your learning with others.
- Ask yourself this question: "OK! I have arrived! Now, how can I think and dream bigger?" or "What next?"

Take time to review your list of goals. Is there anything that you no longer want to do, be, or have? Perhaps there are new items that you would like to add to your list. It is okay not to want what you originally put on your list because as you change so do your wants and needs for fulfillment. You might create a check point in which you need to check and review your goals it could be three months, six months, or a year down the road from the time you first create your goal.

As your needs and wants change, update your vision. Redefine your life purpose and re-create your GPS Dashboard. GPS Dashboards can be updated every three to six months or even yearly. It all depends on how quickly you achieve the goals you have set for yourself.

When you reach your goals celebrate your success in a big way by making sure you acknowledge yourself for your focus and discipline in going after what you want.

CELEBRATE YOUR STRENGTHS AND WINS

We celebrate many milestones in our lives like birthdays, graduations, and a person's life when they die; but do we celebrate all the things we accomplish along the way. There are many things that you do each and every day that you can be grateful for and celebrate. You may take for granted what it is that makes you the person you are.

What makes you unique? When you discovered your GPS True Calling in the earlier chapters, you looked upon your strengths. You looked at what people complimented you on and what you felt you were good at. How do you honor your strengths and successes?

Here are 10 ways in which you can honor your strengths and successes:

- Acknowledge your achievements by keeping a success record. This can be a file of e-mails, letters, cards and pictures celebrating your successes or wins in life.

- Send yourself an e-mail or an e-card to congratulate yourself on your achievement.

- Take a picture of yourself alongside your accomplishment. You may have a picture with your children. It may be a photo of you accepting an award or medal.

- Write paid in full on one of your debts with a happy face and the words—Thank You!

- Take a day off and spend time doing what you love with no cell phone and or computer to distract you.

- Do a happy dance.

- Treat yourself to a massage after a reaching a distance you have been striving for in your running or walking program.

- Call someone and share your achievement.

- If you have reached your ideal weight, you may want treat yourself to a new outfit.

- Look yourself in the mirror and say "You did a great job. Thank you!"

What's Next for Me?

You can do this exercise alone or with someone that you trust. If you choose to do the exercise alone, here are the instructions:

1. Write down a goal that you have just completed.
2. Ask yourself "what's next for me?"
3. Write this answer down under the goal.
4. Now ask yourself "now what's next for me?"
5. Again, write this answer down under the previous one.
6. Keep this questioning going a few more times.
7. Take a look at what the paper reveals to you.

This exercise is great for brainstorming new ideas and coming up with new solutions. You can apply this exercise to any area of your life such as your business or your family. In this book, we have challenged you to think bigger. We hope we have also challenged you to reach a higher potential. "What are you going to do next? What are you going to do after that?" By asking yourself "What's next?" Your mind is suddenly triggered to think bigger and more creatively.

Celebrate Your Journey

Celebrating the journey is the best part of life. People get so caught up in going from activity to the next activity that they forget to enjoy the moment in between. There are rest stops and viewpoints along the road. Stop and be fully present in those moments. Let yourself feel the exhilaration of being one with your chosen path. Your power is the road less traveled. There will be bends and forks in

Celebrating your journey along life's highway involves gratitude, giving, and gifting.

the road to represent opportunities for adventure. The adventure will be yours. What will you choose?

Celebrating your journey along life's highway involves gratitude, giving, and gifting. Gratitude is about celebrating the little steps it took to get where you are today, and about feeling purely grateful. When you are grateful for the things that you have in your life you can keep a positive frame of mind and you are less likely to procrastinate. The more grateful you are for the things that you have in your life, the more things that appear in your life to be grateful for. A gratitude journal is just one way in which you can record the things you are grateful for. We encourage you to write down at least five things you are grateful for each day. You can write in the morning when you awaken or write them down just before you go to bed to clear your mind. It is also so helpful to practice saying thank you, not just when someone serves you or holds the door open. When someone lets you in during a traffic jam, say thank you (even if they can't hear you), this provides you with ongoing practice and focus for living from a foundation of gratitude.

Daily Gratitude Journaling Exercise

List five things you are grateful for today. What you are grateful for does not have to be a big event in your life; it can be all the little things that make you live big. Here are some examples from our entries in our gratitude journals.

- running water in my house
- clean clothes to wear
- food on my table
- time spent with my family
- the warmth of my home
- sunshine
- the smell of rain
- a stranger who smiled when they walked past

GPS Appreciation Board

Just like you created a GPS Dashboard that was future focused, you can create a GPS Appreciation Board which captures your key successes, what you are currently grateful for, and what you have accomplished. You can post letters, cards, or small gifts of appreciation that you have received. This is a great reminder to remember that you are appreciated and valued for your gifts and being a part of the journey of others. When you look at this board, be grateful! Having an appreciation board, can keep you motivated to continue on your journey. It also offers a point of reference to remind you that you are on the right track and living your true calling.

SHARE THE ROAD

One of the greatest lessons that people can benefit from is the lesson of giving first and expecting nothing in return. When you give of yourself and share what you know that you have helped someone reach their highest potential. When you help others succeed, they will want to help you succeed. The more we give to others, the more we get in return. You can give in many ways: time, talent, or money. The gift of time is invaluable. When you can give your undivided attention to someone, you make them the center of your world and they feel valued and appreciated.

The more we give to others, the more we get in return.

Do not come from a place of expectation. What we mean by this is if someone gives to you and you feel then you owe them something back in return. Or that someone owes you because you helped them. Sometimes people keep track of their giving and the amount they think they are owed. This creates a different energy in the relationship and actually creates some friction and resistance. Coming purely from a place of giving has a feeling of openness or unconditional giving. When we hope to receive something from someone, it is a perfect opportunity for asking (for your need or how can help someone else) which is also pure, and from the heart.

Your talent may help someone in an area that they do not know much about. They can learn from you and pattern from you what it takes to succeed. Money is always an option with giving. Money then takes the form of a gift. You can gift someone by buying them to a ticket to an event which they may or may not be able to afford. Know that you are helping someone along their journey unconditionally. The impacts may not be immediate but may create a ripple

You can touch someone's life just by being you.

effect in the world around the person helped. If you're asked what they could do in return, to help them, tell them to pay it forward.

By sharing your time, talent, or money with another person you are creating a living legacy. What legacy do you would like to leave? You touch the lives of all the people you encounter. You may have smiled at someone who was lonely or held open a door for someone carrying an armful of groceries. Simple random acts of kindness are part of your legacy.

Every day people are changed by simple gifts. To change lives, you do not need to be a celebrity or in front of thousands of people. You can touch someone's life just by being you. The gifts you bring are simply amazing and do not have the cost great deal of money. People like to be acknowledged, valued, and appreciated. The gifts that often create the greatest impact are the most simple. Think of the people in your life who make a difference. What examples do they share?

We have both used all these tools, together and separately, for many years. Some mentors have taken us under their wings to help us supersize our success. Now we are able to do the same and give back the knowledge we have shared. What good is knowledge if it is not shared?

Those who use these tools really set themselves apart from those who do not have a plan of action. We have numerous examples of these people in our lives. Men and women, even kids who have used some or all of these tools and are now positioned for success, living their best life and getting there in style. Not to toot our own horn but as we get more involved in helping and giving to others, we have champions who want to hop on the journey with us. The same will happen for you.

Another inspirational story that we enjoy is the true story of Johnny the Bagger. Johnny was a grocery bagger who wanted to make a difference in his role at the grocery store. He started handing out slips of paper to customers who came down his grocery line. These slips of paper were called Johnny's Thought of the Day. People loved receiving these positive messages so much that everyone wanted to purchase their groceries in Johnny's lane. His was a simple gesture that made a huge impact.

We often talk enthusiastically about how we can create a tidal wave of goodness and kindness through the actions of creating the ripple effect. What we often see is that one good deed, one kind word, a smile, or the gift of time, extended to others is contagious. What ripple effect will you create today?

Think about the people who have impacted your life and have made a difference in the person you are today. Take some time to write them a letter or make a phone call to let them know about the impact they had in your life. You do not always hear about the impact you have had in another person's life, but when you do, that is truly a gift.

Know When You Have Arrived

Know when you have reached your goal. It is because you took time to be clear on what it was you wanted your best life to look like and made a plan that now you can reap the rewards. Celebrate, be open, and allow yourself to continually grow. Be excited about the next leg of the journey. The wide open highway awaits you . . . and your dreams!

Road Rules to Live By

1. Acknowledge when your goal is achieved; then set new goals.
2. Celebrate your strengths and wins.
3. Challenge yourself to think bigger.
4. Appreciate what you have and share the road with others . . . and enjoy!

Mapping Your Way

1. How has identifying your winning accomplishments kept you motivated?

2. What five things are you grateful for today?

3. How do you recognize when you have reached your goal or destination?

In conclusion:

We wish you well on "GPSing Your Best Life"! The goal is to go for it—to turn on the engine, put the pedal to the metal! We hope this book serves as a good road map as you "take the trip" to do all you can in life. To that end, we share a few final thoughts:

- We are always on a journey, as long as we are alive, the journey continues.

- With success comes challenge, when you see challenge as an opportunity, you can move with more ease and grace.

- Learning moments arise for us to grow, and to help others grow and learn with us.

- Bring the most authentic version of *you*, on your journey.

- You are powerful and have all the resources and gifts that you need.

- Dream big dreams and think big thoughts.

- Live—to your highest potential.

ABOUT THE AUTHORS

CHARMAINE HAMMOND is an international transformational speaker who has presented to more than 60,000 people around the world. Charmaine is a sought-after consultant and facilitator for large industry, corporations, and government and professional associations, helping businesses build inspired, productive, and resilient teams.

She is also the author of the popular, bestselling and award winning book *On Toby's Terms* (Bettie Youngs Book Publishers, 2010), which is in development to become a major motion picture. Charmaine has also authored a book series for children, the first in the series being *Toby the Pet Therapy Dog and His Hospital Friends* (Bettie Youngs Book Publishers, 2011) which is actively utilized in many educational programs. The next in the series, *Toby Says Be a Buddy Not a Bully,* (Bettie Youngs Book Publishers, 2012). Charmaine has written in a number of magazines and for professional industry and association article sites.

Charmaine is the host of three radio shows, and has been featured in a number of magazines including *Human Resources Network, Alberta Health & Safety, Be Fabulous Magazine, Women & Wealth,* and *The Advocate.* She is the founding and board member of the

Evolutionary Business Council. She is the recipient of a number of awards, and actively gives back to the community through her pay it forward programs and her Million Acts of Kindness—Toby's Global Legacy Mission.

She has a master's degree in conflict analysis and management, a BA in social development studies, and diplomas in social work and correctional worker studies. To contact:

www.hammondgroup.biz
www.ontobysterms.com
www.howtosellandmarketyourbook.com

DEBRA KASOWSKI has a BSc in Nursing and has practiced nursing for over seventeen years. She has combined her passion and love of helping people with her professional speaking career to inspire and help people transform their lives. She also leads several workshops and provides personal coaching. She is the founder of the Millionaire Woman Club, a global community of women who are highly motivated and passionate about helping women become "rich from the inside out."

Debra is also a founding member of the Evolutionary Business Council and a transformational speaker who inspires her audiences to take action. She is published in *Today's Business Woman Magazine* and has been featured on the online magazine *Healthy, Wealthy, and Wise,* as well as radio and television media.

Debra and her husband started the "Spirit of Christmas" Shoebox program from one of her bucket list ideas. The program has recently doubled in capacity and provided gifts and breakfast to more than 1,200 children. To contact:

www.debrakasowski.com
www.themillionairewoman.com

Other Books by
Bettie Youngs Book Publishers

On Toby's Terms

Charmaine Hammond

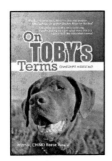

On Toby's Terms is an endearing story of a beguiling creature who teaches his owners that, despite their trying to teach him how to be the dog they want, he is the one to lay out the terms of being the dog he needs to be. This insight would change their lives forever.

Simply a beautiful book about life, love, and purpose. —**Jack Canfield, co-author,** *Chicken Soup for the Soul* **series**

In a perfect world, every dog would have a home and every home would have a dog like Toby! —**Nina Siemaszko, actress,** *The West Wing*

This is a captivating, heartwarming story and we are very excited about bringing it to film. —**Steve Hudis, Producer**

Soon to be a major motion picture!

ISBN: 978-0-9843081-4-9 • $14.95

Toby, the Pet Therapy Dog, and His Hospital Friends

Charmaine Hammond
Illustrated by Rose Anne Prevec

Toby is a big, brown, happy dog. Every week his owner takes him to visit and comfort children who are in the hospital. Follow Toby the therapy dog for a day and see how he makes friends, and makes others happy. Beautifully illustrated, this simple story sends a positive message about community and the importance of kindness and being helpful to others.

ISBN: 978-0-9836045-0-1 • $12.95 US

It Started with Dracula
The Count, My Mother, and Me

Jane Congdon

The terrifying legend of Count Dracula silently skulking through the Transylvania night may have terrified generations of filmgoers, but the tall, elegant vampire captivated and electrified a young Jane Congdon, igniting a dream to one day see his mysterious land of ancient castles and misty hollows. Four decades later she finally takes her long-awaited trip—never dreaming that it would unearth decades-buried memories, and trigger a life-changing inner journey. A memoir full of surprises, Jane's story is one of hope, love—and second chances.

Unfinished business can surface when we least expect it. *It Started with Dracula* is the inspiring story of two parallel journeys: one a carefully planned vacation and the other an astonishing and unexpected detour in healing a wounded heart. **—Charles Whitfield, MD, bestselling author of** *Healing the Child Within*

An elegantly written and cleverly told story. An electrifying read. **—Diane Bruno, CISION Media**

ISBN: 978-1-936332-10-6 • $15.95

Blackbird Singing in the Dead of Night
What to Do When God Won't Answer

Gregory L. Hunt

Pastor Greg Hunt had devoted nearly thirty years to congregational ministry, helping people experience God and find their way in life. Then came his own crisis of faith and calling. While turning to God for guidance, he finds nothing. Neither his education nor his religious involvements could prepare him for the disorienting impact of the experience.

Alarmed, he tries an experiment. The result is startling—and changes his life entirely.

In this most beautiful memoir, Greg Hunt invites us into an unsettling time in his life, exposes the fault lines of his faith, and describes the path he walked into and out of the dark. Thanks to the trail markers he leaves along the way, he makes it easier for us to find our way, too. **—Susan M. Heim, co-author,** *Chicken Soup for the Soul, Devotional Stories for Women*

Compelling. If you have ever longed to hear God whispering a love song into your life, read this book. **—Gary Chapman,** *NY Times* **bestselling author,** *The Love Languages of God*

ISBN: 978-1-936332-07-6 • $15.95

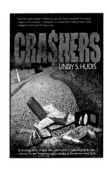

Crashers
A Tale of "Cappers" and "Hammers"

Lindy S. Hudis

The illegal business of fraudulent car accidents is a multi-million dollar racket, involving unscrupulous medical providers, personal injury attorneys, and the cooperating passengers involved in the accidents. Innocent people are often swept into it.

Newly engaged Nathan and Shari, who are swimming in mounting debt, were easy prey: seduced by an offer from a stranger to move from hard times to good times in no time, Shari finds herself the "victim" in a staged auto accident. Shari gets her payday, but breaking free of this dark underworld will take nothing short of a miracle.

A riveting story of love, life—and limits. A non-stop thrill ride. —**Dennis "Danger" Madalone, stunt coordinator for the television series,** *Castle*

ISBN: 978-1-936332-27-4 • $16.95

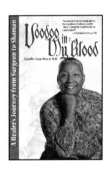

Voodoo in My Blood
A Healer's Journey from Surgeon to Shaman

Carolle Jean-Murat, M.D.

Born and raised in Haiti to a family of healers, US trained physician Carolle Jean-Murat came to be regarded as a world-class surgeon. But her success harbored a secret: in the operating room, she could quickly intuit the root cause of her patient's illness, often times knowing she could help the patient without having to put her under the knife. Carolle knew that to fellow surgeons, her intuition was best left unmentioned. But when the devastating earthquake hit Haiti and Carolle returned to help—she had to acknowledge the shaman she had become.

This mesmerizing story takes us inside the secret world of voodoo as a healing practice, and sheds light on why it remains a mystery to most and shunned by many.

This fascinating memoir sheds light on the importance of asking yourself, "Have I created for myself the life I've meant to live?" —**Christiane Northrup, M.D., author of the** *New York Times* **bestsellers:** *Women's Bodies, Women's Wisdom* and *The Wisdom of Menopause*

"A masterpiece! Truly enlightening. A personal story you won't soon forget." —**Adrianne Belafonte-Bizemeyer**

ISBN: 978-1-936332-05-2 • $24.95 US

DON CARINA
WWII Mafia Heroine

Ron Russell

A father's death in Southern Italy in the 1930s—a place where women who can read are considered unfit for marriage—thrusts seventeen-year-old Carina into servitude as a "black widow," a legal head of the household who cares for her twelve siblings. A scandal forces her into a marriage to Russo, the "Prince of Naples."

By cunning force, Carina seizes control of Russo's organization and disguising herself as a man, controls the most powerful of Mafia groups for nearly a decade. Discovery is inevitable: Interpol has been watching. Nevertheless, Carina survives to tell her children her stunning story of strength and survival.

ISBN: 978-0-9843081-9-4 • $15.95

Living with Multiple Personalities
The Christine Ducommun Story

Christine Ducommun

Christine Ducommun was a happily married wife and mother of two, when—after moving back into her childhood home—she began to experience panic attacks and a series of bizarre flashbacks. Eventually diagnosed with Dissociative Identity Disorder (DID), Christine's story details an extraordinary twelve-year ordeal unraveling the buried trauma of her past and the daunting path she must take to heal from it. Therapy helps to identify Christine's personalities and understand how each helped her cope with her childhood, but she'll need to understand their influence on her adult life.

Fully reawakened and present, the personalities compete for control of Christine's mind as she bravely struggles to maintain a stable home for her growing children. In the shadows, her life tailspins into unimaginable chaos—bouts of drinking and drug abuse, sexual escapades, theft and fraud—leaving her to believe she may very well be losing the battle for her sanity. Nearing the point of surrender, a breakthrough brings integration.

A brave story of identity, hope, healing and love.

Reminiscent of the Academy Award-winning *A Beautiful Mind,* this true story will have you on the edge of your seat. Spellbinding! —**Josh Miller, Producer**

ISBN: 978-0-9843081-5-6 • $16.95

Amazing Adventures of a Nobody

Leon Logothetis

Tired of his disconnected life and uninspiring job, Leon leaves it all behind—job, money, home even his cell phone—and hits the road with nothing but the clothes on his back. His journey from Times Square to the Hollywood sign relying on the kindness of strangers and the serendipity of the open road, inspires a dramatic and life changing transformation.

A gem of a book; endearing, engaging and inspiring. —**Catharine Hamm,** *Los Angeles Times* **Travel Editor**

Leon reaches out to every one of us who has ever thought about abandoning our routines and living a life of risk and adventure. His tales of learning to rely on other people are warm, funny, and entertaining. If you're looking to find meaning in this disconnected world of ours, this book contains many clues. —*Psychology Today*

ISBN: 978-0-9843081-3-2 • $14.95

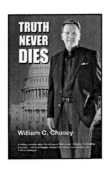

Truth Never Dies

William C. Chasey

A lobbyist for some 40 years, William C. Chasey represented some of the world's most prestigious business clients and twenty-three foreign governments before the US Congress. His integrity never questioned.

All that changed when Chasey was hired to forge communications between Libya and the US Congress. A trip he took with a US Congressman for discussions with then Libyan leader Muammar Qadhafi forever changed Chasey's life. Upon his return, his bank accounts were frozen, clients and friends had been advised not to take his calls.

Things got worse: the CIA, FBI, IRS, and the Federal Judiciary attempted to coerce him into using his unique Libyan access to participate in a CIA-sponsored assassination plot of the two Libyans indicted for the bombing of Pan Am flight 103. Chasey's refusal to cooperate resulted in the destruction of his reputation, a six-year FBI investigation and sting operation, financial ruin, criminal charges, and incarceration in federal prison.

A somber tale, a thrilling read. —**Gary Chafetz, author,** *The Perfect Villain: John McCain and the Demonization of Lobbyist Jack Abramoff*

ISBN: 978-1-936332-46-5 • $24.95

Out of the Transylvania Night

Aura Imbarus

A Pulitzer-Prize entry

"I'd grown up in the land of Transylvania, homeland to Dracula, Vlad the Impaler, and worse, dictator Nicolae Ceausescu," writes the author. "Under his rule, like vampires, we came to life after sundown, hiding our heirloom jewels and documents deep in the earth." Fleeing to the US to rebuild her life, she discovers a startling truth about straddling two cultures and striking a balance between one's dreams and the sacrifices that allow a sense of "home."

Aura's courage shows the degree to which we are all willing to live lives centered on freedom, hope, and an authentic sense of self. Truly a love story! —**Nadia Comaneci, Olympic Champion**

A stunning account of erasing a past, but not an identity. —**Todd Greenfield, 20th Century Fox**

ISBN: 978-0-9843081-2-5 • $14.95

Universal Co-opetition
Nature's Fusion of
Co-operation and Competition

V Frank Asaro

A key ingredient in business success is competition—and cooperation. Too much of one or the other can erode personal and organizational goals. This book identifies and explains the natural, fundamental law that unifies the apparently opposing forces of cooperation and competition. By finding this synthesis point in a variety of situations—from the personal to the organizational—this is the ultimate recipe for individual or group success.

"Your extraordinary book has given me valuable insights." —**Spencer Johnson, author,** *Who Moved My Cheese*

ISBN: 978-1-936332-08-3 • $15.95 US

The Maybelline Story—And the Spirited Family Dynasty Behind It

Sharrie Williams

Throughout the twentieth century, Maybelline inflated, collapsed, endured, and thrived in tandem with the nation's upheavals. Williams, to avoid unwanted scrutiny of his private life, cloistered himself behind the gates of his Rudolph Valentino Villa and ran his empire from a distance. This never before told story celebrates the life of a man whose vision rocketed him to success along with the woman held in his orbit: his brother's wife, Evelyn Boecher—who became his lifelong fascination and muse. A fascinating and inspiring story, a tale both epic and intimate, alive with the clash, the hustle, the music, and dance of American enterprise.

A richly told story of a forty-year, white-hot love triangle that fans the flames of a major worldwide conglomerate. —**Neil Shulman, Associate Producer,** *Doc Hollywood*

Salacious! Engrossing! There are certain stories, so dramatic, so sordid, that they seem positively destined for film; this is one of them. —*New York Post*

ISBN: 978-0-9843081-1-8 • $18.95

The Rebirth of Suzzan Blac

Suzzan Blac

A horrific upbringing and then abduction into the sex slave industry would all but kill Suzzan's spirit to live. But a happy marriage and two children brought love—and forty-two stunning paintings, art so raw that it initially frightened even the artist. "I hid the pieces for 15 years," says Suzzan, "but just as with the secrets in this book, I am slowing sneaking them out, one by one by one." Now a renowned artist, her work is exhibited world-wide.

A story of inspiration, truth and victory.

A solid memoir about a life reconstructed. Chilling, thrilling, and thought provoking. —**Pearry Teo, Producer,** *The Gene Generation*

ISBN: 978-1-936332-22-9 • $16.95

The Morphine Dream

Don Brown with Boston Globe Pulitzer nominated Gary S. Chafetz

At 36, high-school dropout and a failed semi-professional ballplayer Donald Brown hit bottom when an industrial accident left him immobilized. But Brown had a dream while on a morphine drip after surgery: he imagined himself graduating from Harvard Law School (he was a classmate of Barack Omaba) and walking across America. Brown realizes both seemingly unreachable goals, and achieves national recognition as a legal crusader for minority homeowners. This intriguing tale of his long walk—both physical and metaphorical—is an amazing story of loss, gain and the power of perseverance.

"An incredibly inspirational memoir." —**Alan M. Dershowitz, professor, Harvard Law School**

ISBN: 978-1-936332-25-0 • $16.95 US

Hostage of Paradox: A Memoir

John Rixey Moore

A profound odyssey of a college graduate who enlists in the military to avoid being drafted, becomes a Green Beret Airborne Ranger, and is sent to Vietnam where he is plunged into high-risk, deep-penetration operations under contract to the CIA—work for which he was neither specifically trained nor psychologically prepared, yet for which he is ultimately highly decorated. Moore survives, but can't shake the feeling that some in the military didn't care if he did, or not. Ultimately he would have a 40-year career in television and film.

A compelling story told with extraordinary insight, disconcerting reality, and engaging humor. —**David Hadley, actor, China Beach**

ISBN: 978-1-936332-37-3 • $24.95

The Law of Attraction for Teens
How to Get More of the Good Stuff, and Get Rid of the Bad Stuff!

Christopher Combates

Whether it's getting better grades, creating better relationships with your friends, parents, or teachers, or getting a date for the prom, the Law of Attraction just might help you bring it about. It works like this: Like attracts like. When we align our goals with our best intentions and highest purpose, when we focus on what we want, we are more likely to bring it about. This book will help teens learn how to think, act, and communicate in the positive way.

ISBN: 978-1-936332-29-8 • $14.95

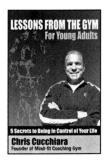

Lessons from the Gym for Young Adults
5 Secrets to Being in Control of Your Life

Chris Cucchiara

Do you lack self-confidence or have a difficult time making decisions? Do you ever have a tough time feeling a sense of purpose and belonging? Do you worry that you don't measure up? Or that you're doing what other people want of you, instead of what you want?

Growing up, Chris Cucchiara felt the same, until he joined a gym. The lessons he learned helped him gain the confidence he needed to set and achieve goals. In *Lessons from the Gym for Yourg Adults,* Chris shares his experiences and powerful insights and shows you how to:

- develop mental toughness (a life without fear, stress, and anger);
- develop an attitude to get and stay healthy and fit;
- build an "athlete for life" mentality that stresses leadership and excellence as a mindset; and,
- stay motivated, and set and achieve goals that matter.

ISBN: 978-1-936332-38-0 • $14.95 US

Fastest Man in the World

Tony Volpentest
Foreword by Ross Perot

Tony Volpentest was born without hands and feet—a condition so rare it does not have a name. Doctors said he would never be able to walk without prosthetics or special accommodations. Tony proved them all wrong.

In high school he took up the least likely sport for someone without feet—track. Through sheer will and perseverance he went from last place in every race to the pinnacle of his sport—becoming a gold medalist and world-record holder—a tour de force who dominated the sprint distances. Along the way, he gained the admiration and respect of others considered great: Ross Perot, Michael Johnson, Joe DiMaggio, Lou Ferrigno.

Tony's incredible story is more than one about sports. It is about the potential of the human spirit. It is about finding the gifts in life's inevitable roadblocks. Tony's motto is "If you can dream it, you can achieve it."

This inspiring story is about the thrill of victory to be sure—winning Olympic Gold—but it is also a reminder about human potential: the ability to push ourselves beyond the ledge of imagination, and to develop grit that fuels indefatigable determination. Simply a powerful story. —**Charlie Huebner, United States Olympic Committee**

ISBN: 978-1-936332-00-7 • $16.95

Diary of a Beverly Hills Matchmaker

Marla Martenson

Marla takes her readers for a hilarious romp through her days in an exclusive matchmaking agency. From juggling the demands of out-of-touch clients and trying to meet the capricious demands of an insensitive boss to the ups and downs of her own marriage with a husband who doesn't think that she is "domestic" enough, Marla writes with charm and self-effacement about the universal struggles of finding the love of our lives—and knowing it.

Martenson's irresistible quick wit will have you rolling on the floor. —**Megan Castran, international YouTube Queen**

ISBN: 978-0-9843081-0-1 • $14.95

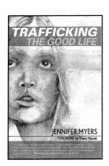

Trafficking the Good Life

Jennifer Myers

A Desperate Search for Self Leads to
Downfall and Ultimate Redemption

An all-American, midwestern farm girl, Jennifer Myers had worked hard toward a successful career as a dancer in Chicago. But just as her star was rising, she fell for the kingpin of a drug trafficking operation. Drawn to his life of excitement, she soon acquiesced to driving marijuana across the country, making easy money she stacked in shoeboxes and spent like an heiress.

Steeped inside moral ambiguity, she sought to cleanse her soul with the guidance of spiritual gurus and New Age prophets—to no avail. Only time in a federal prison made her face up to and understand her choices. It was there, at rock bottom, that she discovered that her real prison was the one she had unwittingly made inside herself and where she could start rebuilding a life of purpose and ethical pursuit.

"Enthralling...and dramatic." —**Dennis Sobin, Director, Safe Streets Arts Foundation**

ISBN: 978-1-936332-67-0 • $18.95

In bookstores everywhere, online, Espresso, or from the publisher, Bettie Youngs Books:

www.BettieYoungsBooks.com

To contact:
info@BettieYoungsBooks.com

Bettie Youngs Books

*We specialize in MEMOIRS
. . . books that celebrate
fascinating people and
remarkable journeys*

VISIT OUR WEBSITE AT
www.BettieYoungsBooks.com

CPSIA information can be obtained at www.ICGtesting.com
Printed in the USA
BVOW012328081112

305048BV00001B/4/P